Revolution in Consciousness

By the same author

The Magic Tarot: Vehicle of Eternal Wisdom

Revolution in Consciousness

Frédéric Lionel

Routledge & Kegan Paul
London, Boston, Melbourne and Henley

Originally published in France as Une autre Conscience pour un âge
nouveau
© *Editions Robert Laffont, S.A., Paris, 1983*

*This translation first published in 1984
by Routledge & Kegan Paul plc*

39 Store Street, London WC1E 7DD, England

9 Park Street, Boston, Mass. 02108, USA

*464 St Kilda Road, Melbourne,
Victoria 3004, Australia and*

*Broadway House, Newtown Road,
Henley-on-Thames, Oxon RG9 1EN, England*

*Photoset in 11 on 13 pt Palatino by
Kelly Typesetting Ltd, Bradford-on-Avon, Wilts
and printed in Great Britain by
T.J. Press (Padstow) Ltd, Padstow, Cornwall*

© *Routledge & Kegan Paul 1984*

ISBN 0–7102–0066–8

Contents

Preface

A psychological revolution is taking place in the West, fostered by the confusion of today's world. It is impossible to tell what the consequences will be.

Hopes for the birth of a new era are becoming widespread. Although people long for this era to be different, they lack a clear idea of what is at stake, and the mere dream is not sufficient to make it a reality. The aspiration for a future full of promise reflects an eternal human quest for happiness, which seems ever elusive.

We may therefore ask: does our civilization encourage such a quest, leading to happiness?

In this century, which considers itself rational, scientific and logical, humanity gropes its way along the roads of existence, stumbling against obstacles which it has placed in its own path.

Struggles, confrontations, violence and fanaticism create a pathological state of mind which makes it difficult to find solutions for the problems of this modern age now drawing to a close.

The new age which will supplant the old one can only be beneficial if Western man integrates the power gained from his knowledge, in which he takes pride, into a different vision of the Truths of Life. This requires another state of consciousness.

We must understand that the dark clouds gathering on the horizon of a disoriented world are the result of our own negligence and that the time has come to prove that the innumerable prophets announcing disaster are mistaken.

Astrologically, the precessional movement of the solar system is causing it to leave the zodiac sign of Pisces and enter that of Aquarius.

Does this indicate a turning point which may produce a twilight of the gods or, on the contrary, will it culminate in a cycle of human achievement?

As the heirs of Alexandria, Athens, Rome and Nazareth, do we in the West have reason for optimism for a bright future?

Will the degradation of essential values and the spread of licentiousness undermine our civilization, or instead can we reverse the trend and transform into hope the fear which has humanity in its grip?

It is not just the happiness of humanity which is in question, but its survival. Although the idea of a possible reversal may be met with scepticism, we ought to consider it and, even more importantly, promote it.

'The evils which devour men are the fruits of their choices', Pythagoras said. If such is the case, are we able to choose wisely? In order to respond to this essential question we must examine the situation with care.

What are the reasons for an apparent decline in our civilization? What are the causes behind it? Must we give up hope or can we work instead towards the creation of a new 'Renaissance'?

Western man's long past, his great experience and his tradition – one of the oldest in the world, which originated in the Mediterranean – summon him to take up the challenge.

Undoubtedly, the task is an arduous one, since destructive folly seems to triumph everywhere.

Will the new era, holding out the promise of a glorious dawn, keep its pledge? Will men and women, for too long prey to the violence of their passions, allow a glimmer of hope to filter through their own contradictions?

A moment always comes when adversaries, tired of useless struggle, discover Intelligence, the daughter of Wisdom. It is she who can bring the conflict to an end. The hour of Intelligence has perhaps not yet struck, but the spirit of the times is accelerating her arrival.

To accept or abdicate its mission – such is the dilemma the West must face.

The choice is crucial. The future of civilization depends upon it!

CHAPTER 1

The Mysterious Mirror
of Pure Truth

It is said that the world is the mysterious mirror of pure truth. Let us contemplate its reflection, while keeping our fears, our preconceived notions and our fixed ideas from clouding the mirror's surface.

Setting aside all intellectual, familial, social or religious influences, let us see things as they are in their essence. This is no easy task! Confusion plays havoc with the problems we would like to resolve. We classify them into categories, separating them from the context in which they originated, and then we pretend that order has been established. Such pretences lead to false solutions.

The world is confused and in a state of turmoil. However, the discovery of the reasons for such confusion and turmoil, as well as for the fear which these generate, can enable us to reach a higher vantage point which encompasses the past, the present and the future, and can help us to see things as they are essentially.

We proceed from the past; we exist in the present; and our actions determine the future. It follows that the new age will be what we make it and that we must therefore assume our responsibilities. In order to do so, we must contemplate without illusion the reflections of the mysterious mirror which is the world, distancing ourselves from its confusion in order to recognize the underlying causes. Only then will we be able to link the various aspects together in order to discover the web upon which those three sisters of Fate, the Parcae, weave the destiny of humanity.

The events and themes in the following chapters do not follow any chronological order, since they are merely illustrations of a constant evolution. It is the meaning of this evolution which we must understand. It continues without interruption, but since our ignorance causes us to act without taking it into account, we become the victims of our own choices.

If, when contemplating the events of our world, we recognize the thread establishing the relationship among them, then we are led from one thing to all the others, just as pearls linked by a string form a necklace.

We speak of a sense of history and not of a sense of evolution – a convenient way to replace our responsibility with an illusion and to ignore the Laws of Life. When we claim to understand history and to accept its constraints, failing to realize that it is our own actions which determine history, we deny the obvious. Such a denial is all the more regrettable since history is a fascinating chronicle of our own evolution.

If through ignorance, ambition or lack of awareness, our human endeavours are opposed to the Law of Life, Life's dynamism will overturn the obstacles in its path. Wars, revolutions, epidemics and catastrophes are merely the consequences of an absence of foresight on our part; they force us, as a result of our experiences, to discover our lack of insight and the reason for our folly.

'It is not my will that I do, but that of my Father', Jesus said. The will of the Father is the expression of the Law, and consequently it is an integral part of the annals of history.

When truly inspired human beings actively participate in the movement of evolution, civilizations are created which express the multiple facets of humanity's original genius.

However, every human achievement deteriorates eventually, and today, through the action of individuals calling themselves civilized, the symptoms of decadence are multiplying.

This decadence may not be inevitable, since in every part of the world an authentic aspiration is emerging. Although unavoidable excesses are most regrettable, even these demonstrate the vitality of an essential quest, that of understanding the meaning of the human journey on earth.

Even in the darkest hours hope is possible, since an inexhaustible dynamism, the sap of Life, pulsates (and acts) in the crucible of the world. When, thanks to the understanding of the awakened, intelligent human being, visible actions as well as their sometimes invisible results are in perfect symbiosis with the living forces of nature, they harmoniously restore whatever seems out of order. We may act in full attunement with these forces, fulfilling thereby our human vocation and joining our own creative forces to those which manifest themselves in the cosmos. Such is our predestination!

In order to convince ourselves of this possibility as our cycle draws to a close, let us explore the historical developments of the last two thousand years which culminated in our civilization.

The West seeks itself without knowing itself, without being aware of the truths which could serve as a foundation for its forward movement.

As ideas conflict with one another, colliding and only seldom coinciding, minds are filled with doubt.

Doubt can show us the path to truth, provided it

escapes the despotism of ideas which crystallize opinions and thereby influence human actions.

'The greatest human quest,' Kant suggested, 'is to know what one must do in order to become a human being.'

Our rejection of such a fundamental statement is evident from our reactions, which take the form of an avalanche of theories and dogmas claiming to solve all problems.

In a century which has witnessed the release of atomic energy, we persist in clinging to mental projections which have proved themselves false. We hold fast to our beliefs because we lack the necessary courage to abandon them.

The fundamental error of theories, dogmas and systems results from an ambiguity concerning the proper meaning of two words which are in no way synonymous: 'to exist' and 'to be'.

In fact, the reality of being manifests itself in existence, since man is a being who gives existence in his body to a series of physical, emotional and mental mechanisms which make possible the expression of Life which animates him.

He must therefore ensure that his existence unfolds under conditions favourable to the harmonious functioning of his organism, and he must also remain aware that his means of expression should reflect his essential aspirations. Well-being, which differs from 'existing well', determines the development of his faculties and, as a result, leads to mastery of his destiny.

Failing to accept his 'indivi-duality' – that is, his indivisible duality, the duality of his physical nature and his spiritual aspirations – man behaves inconsistently on all levels. His activity is no longer adapted to a century in which scientists try to represent in one formula the mystery of mankind and its universal reality.

If we are to follow the trend of evolution, we must create the foundations for a harmonious order suited to the aspirations of those who reject barren forms of organization based exclusively upon efficiency and profit.

Such order can only be achieved through a fundamental transformation of our thought mechanisms, and therefore through a true psychological revolution.

This revolution is essential if a Western 'Renaissance' is to occur. Such a Renaissance could reveal to us a human vocation which gives meaning to existence and offers hope to a generation in search of itself – a generation inclined to flee the void within, which it imagines all too often can be filled with drugs, violence or total indifference.

We, the older generation, must correct their error. It does little good to forbid certain types of attitudes or behaviour. Rather, the experience of a long evolution can point to intangible truths.

From our modern perspective, we are now aware only of the senseless divisions of ancient Greece and their uselessness. On the other hand, we accept with pride the subtle influences of a civilization from which ours was born. Our awareness of this fact may help us discover a teaching which merits consideration.

We retain in our soul the divine proportions revealed by Greek art. We remember that the Pythagorean spirit illuminated the sky of Attica five centuries before the birth of Christ. We admire the ancient temples or their remains, and we can imagine the splendours of the sanctuaries where religion elaborated its mysteries in order to give the faithful a foretaste of celestial beatitude.

We would not be what we are without reference to the pinnacles of human achievement which constitute our sacred inheritance.

May we play our part in enriching it.

CHAPTER 2

Humanism and Liberty

Grandiose and tragic, sublime and sordid are the heights and depths of the human epic. Its kaleidoscopic aspects must be transcended if we are to discover a Reality beyond appearance.

The use of clear and precise words appropriate to the spirit of our times may enable us to discover the deep meaning and the magic of a Tradition which includes the quintessence of a very long human experience. Such a discovery may help us transform the universal anguish into hope for a splendid future.

Above all, the Tradition is the link which unites yesterday with today. It is the Law which indicates the path leading from what has been towards what shall be. Since everything existing is the fruit of the past and the seed of the future, everything bears the imprint of evolution. Evolution manifests a dynamic universal energy, an inexhaustible vital flux which seems to follow a guiding principle, since ever better-adapted forms replace those which vanish in the eternity of time.

Tradition is therefore not a system. It is not a theory, and it can be found on the heights of Tibet as well as in the imposing mass of the Pyramids, in standing stones worn

6

with age as well as in the heart of the sanctuary of the Church of the Nativity.

Rich in teachings, our cycle with all its confusions has produced one of its jewels, humanism, which can in no way be considered a mere collection of intellectual or philosophical tendencies, but is rather a development centering on man. Understood in this way, humanism is an innermost discovery of human capacities, human reason and human development.

Humanism implies harmony as well as the awareness of a universality which renders any sterile classification arbitrary, since it masks the enfoldment of phenomena within each other and the relationships which make them dependent upon one another.

Humanism can only exist when total liberty permits the expression of the greatest originality developed to the point of genius. Humanism as such is the expression of 'Primordial Liberty' manifested on all levels, a liberty which is, however, subject to essential notions we must respect if we wish to avoid violating our own nature, which reflects cosmic harmony.

In putting the cart before the horse – in other words, in seeking a conclusion before demonstrating the soundness of its foundations – we may state that the vocation of the West was, and remains, the expression of a humanism which considers man the measure of all things, since man in his body is the mirror of a transcendental Order.

This century's preference for excess over moderation is not in itself proof of an abdication of responsibility, since civilization has always followed a saw-toothed pattern of peaks and troughs reflecting the development of human genius.

Many minds are occupied by a search for the causes of today's visible decadence, and these causes, often subtle, merit close attention. We must proceed by stages and avoid relying upon false notions which may preclude an objective approach.

Despite the fact that the signs of a new age are becoming apparent, such an age will only keep its promise if spiritual energies are integrated into the conquests of science and modern technology. In our proud belief that science has an answer for everything, we have neglected Spirit.

Spirit is making a sensational reappearance in the very heart of the most advanced theories of basic research. Science is approaching the domain of metaphysics as it dissolves matter and delves into the world of the infinitely small, which defies rational logic.

Nothing remains before the observer but a whirlwind of energies, which he himself is. Confronted with the uncertainty principle which modern physics has established as a postulate, he is forced to change completely the image he has had of the world and of himself.

He realizes, or should realize, that the age of Aquarius will witness the blending of science and Eternal Wisdom, far too long neglected. He must also understand that his own civilization follows other civilizations of stupendous achievement.

The civilization of the Pharaohs in particular has profoundly influenced the spiritual evolution of the West. Two thought currents have transmitted the great themes of Egyptian initiation to us. One is represented by Moses, who guided the tribes of Israel toward the Promised Land and entrusted to them the Ark of the Covenant, containing the essence of the Tradition. The other derives from Pythagoras and other Hellenic philosophers, who also drew upon the treasures of revealed wisdom in ancient Egypt.

An overview of human evolution should make it possible to discover the essential aspects of an experience which, once properly understood, could help humanity avoid numerous pitfalls on its journey. To keep alive the essentials of a Tradition reflecting this experience is to place signposts at the intersections of the roads travelled by humanity.

Let us therefore turn back to the past, to Egypt, the radiant centre of a civilization producing artistic and symbolic achievements which speak a timeless language. Her pyramids are the key to a spiritual geometry. Her myths make the unknowable accessible; her astrology reveals the links which unite man to the cosmos; and the alchemy born on her soil has greatly fostered the development of modern science.

These examples, among many others, illustrate the richness of a heritage all too often discarded. It is not possible here to study its multiple facets in depth. However, we can attempt to contemplate our world from above so as to discern the essential aspects of a Tradition pointing the way to 'initiation'; that is, to a new beginning.

Even a brief examination of the 'whys' and 'hows' of the human sojourn on earth could furnish precious clues derived from our ancient past, and these therefore deserve attention.

At certain turning points in history it becomes apparent that the legitimate heirs of a discarded legacy may discover that a particular thought current is alien to them, not due to any failure on their part, but rather because of their ignorance. Blinded by the promises of triumphant science, they have forgotten that the language of an ancient tradition differs from that accepted by the majority of people who have become estranged from this tradition.

However, the aspiration to partake of the riches in Ali Baba's cave remains, although it is often unconscious. As

André Labarthe has said: 'The only part of Reality to be revealed by immediate phenomenology is a fictitious world which blinds people through daily contact.'

It is therefore necessary to go beyond immediate phenomenology to perceive what lies behind it. Consequently, there is good reason to abandon all preconceived notions and to approach the problems of our times in full objectivity.

CHAPTER 3

A Short Review of the Origins

'Everything moves in the heart of the Impassive One,' claimed the Ancients, 'by the sublime and awesome magic of rhythm.'

Rhythm, a manifestation of the movement of life, fills space, and everything existing is subject to its law which, by its very movement, joins that which seems separated.

The sun rises and sets. Noise grows louder or softer, and day replaces night as night replaces day, in the rhythm of eternity.

To pick a flower is to reach the stars, as modern science illustrates, since the energy fields of the least particle vibrate in unison with the universe.

Whoever speaks of vibration is referring to rhythm, a succession of alternations varying only in frequency.

Today, engineers can discover techniques to create a perfect balance of proportions, which thereby manifest a harmonious logic linking functional form to the canons of beauty. This symbiosis illustrates the consistency of the laws of nature on all levels.

The incessant interactions of successive alternations manifest the transforming pulsation of radiant energy in a universe which is in a process of continual change.

Pythagoras, wishing to make perceptible the supreme

order which produces constant adaptations to external requirements, in the nucleii of atoms as well as in molecules, cells and even worlds, named the universe 'cosmos,' a Greek word meaning order and harmony.

The adepts of the great alchemical art preferred the name of Athanor, a term designating the crucible of transformations.

'Man,' stated the alchemists, 'is a microcosm, a faithful reflection of the macrocosm, and he must achieve within himself the fundamental transformation which opens up, through the transcendence of conceptual limitations, the gates of immortality.'

The vital pulsation produced by the harmonious or discordant interaction of rhythms occurs everywhere and in everything. Rhythm has a frequency which can be expressed in numbers. Numbers, elevated to the level of symbols, become in this way a link between supreme order and its expression.

Today, science is rediscovering the Pythagorean mystery of numbers, which has profoundly influenced the evolution of the West. Energy quanta, axiomatics and transfinite numbers in modern science confirm the teachings of the Sage of Samos.

Although we do not intend to enter deeply into the philosophy of numbers, we may admire the power of simple relationships which determine harmony in the realms of music, art or architecture as well as in nature.

As evolution progresses, nature is transformed according to each historical period by means of human actions which foster such a transformation. Although the Celtic forests and the mythical Hyperborea disappeared, Druidic wisdom fortunately survived in Hellas. There, the pure hero Bel Eol could be rediscovered in the majesty of Apollo, appropriately named the

Hyperborean, and the god Ogmios presided as Logos over the unfoldment of the Word. Ogmios was the god of eloquence in Gaul, and in Greece the term 'Logothetos' referred to a person who delivers a speech. The Word is Life; human speech is a reflection of the Word, and this consideration should inspire us to weigh our words with more care.

The Orphic and Eleusinian Mysteries perpetuated the initiation conferred upon the adepts in the temples of ancient Pharaonic Egypt. The term 'initiation' has often been misunderstood. It referred to a teaching or, even more accurately, to an introduction to the laws of nature governing the visible and invisible worlds – an introduction which made possible a new beginning based upon the wisdom derived from Cognizance.* Such wisdom is reflected in the meaningful words engraved upon the pediment of the temple at Delphi: 'Know yourself, and you will know the universe and the gods.'

Although the influence of this sanctuary was tremendous, already a new era could be discerned on the horizon. The task of this era would be to make man worthy of assuming his destiny by imparting to him the teaching of Jesus, whose words, 'I am the Way, the Truth and the Life', need no elaboration.

Before we enter the Christian era, let us pause briefly in Egypt. We may agree with Plotinus, the Alexandrian scholar, that the sages of Egypt attained a highly developed science, accessible to those philosophers who could decipher the symbols, metaphors for eternally valid ideas.

They believed that this understanding would permit them to rise gradually above the world of multiplicity

---

* Cognizance unites knowledge with understanding, so that we know how best to use knowledge under given circumstances.

to attain primordial unity, thereby gaining access to supreme harmony through their love of Cognizance.

Plotinus, aware of a tradition deeply rooted in the 'mysterial' science – the science of the mysteries of nature which the initiated priests of ancient Egypt preserved and transmitted – wanted to be the interpreter of this wisdom through the use of a dialectic similar to that of Plato.

Our rapid review of the origins now finds its true significance, by assigning to the magic of ancient Wisdom its proper dimension.

Magic, in the ancient sense of the term, was the binding force holding together a theocracy, the authority of which endured over many centuries. Magical action was made possible by Cognizance of the laws governing the visible and invisible worlds.

The magic of one period finds without doubt its equivalent in the science of another; science can achieve the same wonders, although on another level and through other means.

The West has certainly succeeded in making this equivalence a reality, which has been achieved through the continual development of mental capacities. Proud of his intellect, rejecting with scorn everything which escapes his observation, Western man has failed to integrate the revealed science of ancient times into contemporary science.

For this reason, most of the keys to a magical form of medicine have been lost, although they are being rediscovered today in what is termed alternative healing.

The complementary aspects of classical medicine and alternative medicine are converging, joining one another in a vision encompassing the physical, psychological and spiritual realms of the patient.

A Short Review of the Origins

The modern medical paradigm – in other words, medicine in its essentials – accepts the idea that an individual is linked to his environment and that his well-being is determined by a harmonious balance which can be restored, if he is the victim of a disease, by a change of attitude towards the illness.

The acceptance of his ordeal enables dynamic forces to emerge which, when properly channelled by an able practitioner, will help the patient to heal himself with a variety of available methods.

Allopathy, homeopathy, psychology and healing by means of the body's energy fields are powerful complementary approaches for restoring bodily order and producing a normal state called health.

Referring to our earlier statements concerning Egyptian magic, we may stress that it adopted many forms. Tantra was a sexual magic originating at Tantyris,* the ancient name for Denderah, known for the zodiac in its temple. Although astrology was introduced into Egypt from Chaldea, its magical power derived from initiated priests in the land of the Pharaohs who were able to elevate it to the level of an art.

Alchemy, originating in the land of Chem, the ancient name for Egypt, has exerted a timeless fascination. The fact that kings, emperors, popes and saints were alchemists would seem to indicate that the Philosopher's Stone, the goal of the Great Work, is more than just an illusion.

We have already spoken of the mystery of numbers. When understood in this way, numbers become a meditation revealing the link which unites the Word to its unfoldment.

* The goddess Bastid (with a cat's head) was the goddess of sacred prostitution in temples. Eroticism was meant to lead to the sublimation of sexuality. Tantra in the oriental sense came later.

The magic of art was the expression of a hieratic and sacred tradition transmitting the secret of forms, gestures and symbols, which are the outer manifestations of the magical power of beauty.

In the temple, it was considered a religious act to give oneself up to this magic which aroused the soul's emotion in the presence of the splendours of the unknowable.

Every civilization needs art in order to define itself and, in this realm, Pharaonic civilization has left us remnants of great distinction.

Egyptian art, unequalled in perfection, transmits a message which transcends time and space. Although it is very different from the art which ultimately flourished in Hellas, the Greek miracle owes to Egypt the vitality that allowed it to blossom.

Despite the multiplicity of styles and different means of expression, medieval art, as well as Renaissance and modern art, transmits a pure tradition which has made goodness, truth and beauty the foundation of human creation.

How indeed can inner life or dreams, surging up from the depths, be expressed if not by art, a wordless language which translates what is felt before being thought?

Art requires 'Primordial Liberty'. For this reason it reflects the spirit of each age, without ever being constricted by rigid canons. In Egypt initiated priests taught artists and artisans who, it may be noted, belonged to the same guild. Although hieratic art had to respect forms and gestures, the artist or artisan had the responsibility of interpreting them in a personally original way.

As guardians of the tradition revealed by their forebears, they were supposed to create works approaching the perfection of Ra, the manifest solar god.

It is scarcely possible to conclude our brief exploration of ancient Egypt without mentioning the pyramids. Despite the fact that they are the most studied of monuments, they remain extremely mysterious. They may have been occult keys to metaphysical mathematics rather than mere tombs.

Our intention is certainly not to take sides in the debate between Egyptologists and pyramidologists. The former only accept historical facts or observable data, whereas the latter seek to decipher the metaphysical, astrological or initiatory symbolism. It is perhaps a vain quarrel, since the two points of view can be perfectly reconciled.

It seems difficult to imagine that six million tons of rock – for such is the estimate for the Cheops pyramid – could have been assembled with such incredible care, hoisted to such unbelievable heights, and oriented in such an amazing fashion merely to serve as a sepulchre for a king, even a divinized Pharaoh.

On the symbolic level the adept – that is, the one admitted to Cognizance – followed a pyramidal progression upward from the square of the base, which represented the world of limits or the framework of existence, to the peak, which represented that which is without limits: the culmination, the Omega point.

Once he had attained this point of Cognizance, the adept, now initiated, master of his destiny and free of all limitations, was considered ready to manifest himself in the regions where the immortals dwell.

The Pharaoh was the living example, having attained perfection after innumerable existences.

Initiation as practised in the temples had a scientific foundation, since it was based upon the Cognizance of the Laws of Nature which enabled one to act in accordance with a Wisdom Tradition deriving from Cognizance.

Let us end this brief visit to the land of the Pharaohs by noting that every action based upon Wisdom requires a choice, a choice which can only be exercised in full liberty. Liberty is thus the foundation of every civilization. When reduced to a political value, it is degraded or suppressed. True liberty, constantly being reborn from its own ashes, is not in any sense something which stirs the masses. It is an inner liberty which, correctly understood, is not only the essence of Spirit, but also the Essence of all civilization.

CHAPTER 4

Royal Alchemy – from which the New Human Being will be Born

Every mission consists of a freely accepted commitment based upon a vocation which must first be recognized.

The confusion of the modern world falsifies the understanding required for such a recognition. Contemporary technology ought to serve man without arousing any fear that it may help blow up the planet.

False notions abound, serving as justifications for choices dictated by theoretical, sociological, political or pseudo-philosophical considerations – in other words, by ideologies raised to the status of dogma.

Confronted with problems beyond our competence, we watch the confusion grow and, since we lack the serenity conferred by inner peace, we alternate between Scylla and Charybdis, between port and starboard on the vessel of our destiny. However, we do not change course.

We are blinded by existential duality, unaware that beyond it we may discover a transcendental reality revealing the fundamental Law of Life to which we are meant to submit.

We will only succeed in such an endeavour by freeing ourselves from all psychological barriers formed by preconceived ideas, impulsive reactions and prejudices,

19

since these are based upon beliefs which must be abandoned if we are to master our destiny. Goethe was certainly thinking about these barriers when through Faust he said: 'Only he deserves liberty who knows how to conquer it daily.'

We are constantly faced by the obvious fact that lack of serenity produces reactions instead of actions based upon free choice.

'Isn't free choice an illusion?' a timid soul might ask, referring to fatality or 'karma', a Sanskrit word for the 'energies of accomplishment' which manifest themselves as effects of unwittingly provoked causes.

Such statements, based upon poorly understood notions, result in erroneous interpretations of the term 'liberty'. This term is given a political or sociological meaning, when in fact its true value is metaphysical. Liberty is too often confused with licence, and attempts are made to incite the masses while claiming to defend it. Politicians, union leaders, dictators and revolutionaries of all persuasions write 'liberty' on their banners, only to suppress it when it becomes contrary to their interests.

When correct ideas are lacking, words take their place. We claim to desire peace without ourselves being peaceful, unaware that war only brings out those contradictions which already exist within everyone. We fight and kill one another, and nothing is resolved. Conflicts survive in latent form, and we forget that violence, used as a means to oppose war, actually provokes war, since violence generates conflict.

To be 'for this' or 'against that' only serves to reinforce fruitless antagonisms. To discover the causes behind the conflict without being carried away by impulsive reactions is to know how to eliminate them through the use of Wisdom.

Correct action needs no justification. It can at times

appear severe, but its severity results from comprehension rather than from reaction, and such comprehension leads to a firm resolve which will discourage any eventual aggressor more successfully than the rattling of weapons.

Because he has failed to recognize his part and his purpose in life, Western man turns to agitation as an outlet for his anguish. He expects to receive everything from outside, preferring to subject himself to governmental organizations so that he may proclaim his rights, forget his duties and refuse to accept his responsibilities. In this way, he increasingly abandons himself to sprawling bureaucratic control while giving up his individuality.

By creating organizations, men implicitly submit to their own requirements, which they subsequently attempt to preserve, afraid to take the initiative – something which they are no longer able to do.

Claiming their rights, social and professional groups oppose one another within nations. Scapegoats abound and terrorism flourishes. Useless struggles exhaust the protagonists and false truces are declared, based upon false notions, false rights and a false liberty.

People are fascinated by false problems and they invent false justifications, which are nothing more than equivocations.

Torrents of blood and tears flood the regions where passions and beliefs confront one another. Beliefs, powerfully supported by theories and systems, face one another in an endless battle, and on both sides the antagonists invoke the justice of the gods, the prophets and the saints in order to mask their confusion, their doubts and their lust for power.

The world is shrouded in a thick fog. The world, however, belongs to us and we can choose our fate, provided we accept our humanity.

Our humanity urges us to reflect upon the warning of Lao Tzu, the Chinese sage, who declared: 'To triumph over others, one must use force. To triumph over oneself, one must *be* forceful.'

'This entire world is nothing but schemes and plots,' exclaims Don Quixote, 'but I am helpless . . .'

No, he is not, provided he acts in full inner liberty, which can only be attained by transcending the corruptible condition of nature.

Different methods of self-realization are directed toward this goal, and these methods are currently experiencing a rapid development in the West. Yoga, meditation, relaxation excercises, breathing therapies and prayer, provided the latter is given a metaphysical significance, all lead to another state of consciousness if they are practised to achieve true awareness rather than a specific goal.

The vocation of the West is to promote this awareness, not as an end in itself, but as a foundation for progress.

Progress can only occur as a function of this other state of consciousness – in other words, through an alchemical transformation, in the highest sense of the term. Royal Alchemy, from which the new human being will be born, is accessible to us today, provided we dare to abandon our obsolete thought mechanisms, provided we understand that everything leads to everything else when we discover the thread establishing the relationship, provided we want what is intended by the Great Plan of Evolution, provided we are innerly silent and turn a deaf ear to the dissonance of the world's confusion.

Then we can listen to the voice which surges up from the depths of being, the voice of the inner master, the voice of awakened consciousness, a reflection of cosmic consciousness.

'Look within yourself,' recommended Marcus

Aurelius, the Roman emperor-sage, 'and you will find the source of true happiness, an inexhaustible source if you look ever deeper.'

The four master words – *dare, understand, will* and *keep silent* – summarize the essential aspects of a humanism which can only exist in full liberty, since it is based upon the harmony resulting from an innermost discovery revealing the path to be followed on our terrestrial journey. Through harmony, everything finds its place and a place can be assigned to everything.

Royal Alchemy requires a transformation which makes possible the manifestation of true Intelligence, the roots of which are plunged into the heart of being. At the centre of the human soul abides the mystery of things, physical as well as spiritual. The human soul participates essentially in the Soul of the World – a poetic metaphor for the movement of life which, through a gigantic inhalation and exhalation, gives rhythm to existence.

At the centre of the human soul, the great book of Cognizance opens up. In order to turn its pages, we must pass through a preliminary stage of self-knowledge – which, according to Demosthenes, is a divine precept.

Saint Teresa of Avila, aware of this, noted the folly of man, imagining that he could enter heaven without first entering within himself to reach true understanding.

When the inner depths have been probed, we reach a second stage which leads to a different way of considering existence.

What seemed important loses its importance; what seemed secondary now seems essential. In short, the visible and invisible relationships with the surrounding world are transformed by an understanding which generates love, not as generosity but as a living communion establishing a link between ourselves and the ambient world.

The third stage culminates in illumination, the ultimate step of the great human adventure on earth. Although it is hardly possible to describe this state of being known to mystics, we are each meant to reach it at the proper time.

Three stages: three processes the alchemists would say, referring to the Emerald Tablet upon which they believed hierophants had engraved entire the 'Royal' science which makes it possible to 'separate the ephemeral from the eternal'.

Such a possibility requires a mind at rest and an ear which is deaf to the noise of the world. The inner ear will then perceive, buried in the shadowy depths of the unconscious, the message of the Word, of Life which animates the Being.

The superior design of existence is implicit in the evolution of things and corresponds to the evolutions of human achievements. The infinite variety of physical, chemical, biological and spiritual combinations offers us an unlimited field of contemplation and meditation leading to creative action, the source of joy and happiness.

Royal Alchemy, requiring the abandonment of all beliefs, all prejudices and all limitations which might hamper a clear comprehension of beings, acts and things, will form the matrix from which the new human being will arise, awakened and aware of the essential.

CHAPTER 5

The Kingdom of Man is Limitless

The awakened human being will no longer try to discover infallible schemes to assure himself of fleeting success, since this threatens to mask the happiness he seeks. He will no longer confuse psychological forces, which give him temporary advantages, with those of the spirit, which allow him to master his destiny. He will no longer resort to subterfuges in order to escape his responsibility; instead, he will accept it. He will therefore be a man reborn, in the true meaning of the term, awakened to the essential realities which will then determine his behaviour.

Since he understands that all forms of belief are attached to doctrines and to prejudices which blind him, he will transcend paralysing concepts, theories and systems which veil the aspirations arising from the depths of the soul and which petrify his thoughts.

Belief has never fostered the expression of love or charity. It produces a deceptive attitude, an inner compromise which reinforces a particular idea that we have of ourselves, of existence and of the world, an idea tainted with preconceived notions.

Only faith, generated at a completely different level from belief, leads to the understanding that the divided

All is still the All, and that we, as a fraction of this Unity, are connected to the cosmos by innumerable links which make us an integral part of Supreme Order and its harmony.

Jesus made use of parables in order to avoid any mental crystallization of his teaching. In fact, the mind must be made fluid in order to permit the upward surge of faith, which transcends all the interpretations we cling to in the hope that our beliefs will make us secure.

'If your faith', said Jesus, 'is only as great as a mustard seed, you will command this mountain to move and it will move, and nothing will be impossible for you.'

Royal Alchemy reveals the Art of Living, not an existential technique. It indicates the path to happiness, which is not a succession of satisfactions, but a state of being. Royal Alchemy, by the transformation it entails, gives us the means to collaborate in the Great Work of Nature as we associate our creative forces with those active in the cosmos.

The adjective 'Royal' is merely used to help the reader avoid confusion between the true alchemists of old and the vulgar makers of gold, charlatans for the most part.

Royal Alchemy is the science of transformations induced by light, the light of Spirit. It produces an essential upsurge which removes obstacles formed by emotional, passionate or instinctive impulses. Then we are able to embrace the truth of the moment, a truth perceived by a previously unknown faculty which does not rely upon concepts provoking desires or fears, whether these are acknowledged or not.

This upsurge helps in daily existence. It occurs when we consciously avoid meaningless words, arbitrary statements or preconceived ideas based upon insufficient observations which are taken as definitive.

Then action, detached from the future and the past,

separated from confusion and turmoil, is like meditation. Meditation is not simply the practice of silence. It is a state of being through which we introduce the soul into a universe where harmony reigns. Centered within, we remain serene in the midst of the world's agitation.

We may wonder why people have meditated since time immemorial. It is because meditation, considered a metaphysical exercise, produces physical and psychological transformations. Through meditation, the barriers formed by concepts or beliefs are dissolved, and it is through this dissolution and the substitution of the faculties of perception that everything changes.

The mention of a new age and of a new human being should not produce in us any sense of satisfaction, as we might then fall prey to imagination. Imagination can produce the belief that everything will work out miraculously in the best of all possible worlds, just as soon as the threshold is crossed separating what has been from what is yet to be.

This belief, like all others, must be discarded. We must prepare, by preparing ourselves, for the emergence of a different consciousness, one which takes into account the conquests of science as well as our deep aspirations, and visualizes a civilization in harmony with the findings of modern physics as well as with the manifestations of spiritual powers entrusted to us, a civilization open to the possibility of future scientific triumphs which can be used for the benefit of wise and intelligent individuals.

It would be absurd to minimize the difficulties of the task, which consists of seeking inspiration in the spirit of scientific progress without renouncing the eternal wisdom experienced by humanity throughout its long past. Such are the necessary conditions for a fundamental transformation. Only a transformation of this kind will enable the new human being to abandon the familiar prison of his conceptual limitations and to undertake an audacious journey of cosmic discovery which will reveal to him the meaning of existence.

Destined to penetrate the immensity of our universe, from the immeasurable depths of the infinitely small to the extreme of the infinitely large, we must realize that both infinities attest to an eternal return. We are meant to give our thought free rein beyond the ephemeral world so that we may pursue the extraordinary adventure of Spirit. Spirit will guide us along the paths of life, turning our attention away from the past and making us understand that life was given to us for a reason. We will then be able to help beautify the Garden of the Creator, which has been entrusted to us for this end.

We will understand that the kingdom of man is without limits and that it extends into the realms where Cosmic Alchemy distils, day after day, the potion of immortality. We will be able to drink it once we have found, in the human crucible, our capacities for discovering the Philosopher's Stone.

From an esoteric perspective, this Stone is self-knowledge which, through deep and abiding faith in life and its magic, reveals an immanent logic in everything existing.

Self-knowledge leads to mastery, since it means penetration into the depths of the unconscious which contains the quintessence of evolutionary experience. The upsurge of self-knowledge is synonymous with an awakening or, as the alchemists would say, with the 'gift of God'.

In this way, if only for an instant, we can perceive reality in movement – 'divine dew', as the adepts of the Great Art would call it – which brings fertility to the barren wastelands of knowledge.

The Stone corresponds to the pure gold of the

alchemists; that is, to the incorruptible and the sacred. The quest for alchemical gold is therefore similar to supreme virtue, which means constant availability of heart and soul as a state of being rather than a moral value.

In all ages, great emissaries have extolled 'Virtue'. This term does not refer to obedience of any rules, but to a submission to the Law of Life. The sacrifices made by these great beings exemplified this. Unfortunately, they were all too often forgotten or misunderstood, and their teachings lost their true meaning.

Man wanders in darkness, seeking light, and since for the past two thousand years the West has been the torch-bearer of the Tradition which is its inheritance, it must avoid squandering the treasure in its care.

The Gospels report that when Andrew, one of the Saviour's disciples, met his brother Simon, he led him to Jesus. Jesus, after considering him a while, said to him: 'You are Simon, son of Jonas. You will be called Peter', in Greek 'Cephas', which means 'rock', and Jesus continued: 'Peter, upon this rock I will build my Church.'

Philosopher's Stone or living rock, two metaphors for a single truth. May we remain faithful to it!

CHAPTER 6

Pandora's Box

To take the path through time and space means leaving behind petrified notions; it means loosening the bonds which attach us to dead things of the past cherished by habit.

To follow the path means realizing that humanity, caught in the constraints of existence, accumulates knowledge without freeing itself from the impediments which keep it prisoner in a web of false interpretations.

Is it possible, when writing the history of a people, to embrace their hopeful dawns and their dark sunsets, their laughter and their tears, when hidden causes escape the most well-intentioned of historians?

Is it possible, when writing the history of the West, to discover the chain of events which have characterized the last few thousand years – merely the continuation of other millennia, the testimony of which cannot be neglected?

Is it possible to discover the proper role of these facts and events in the immense spiral of evolution, and to understand the secret impulses and the hidden thoughts of the individuals who have left their imprint upon history?

Is it possible to perceive the subtle influences upon

those men and women who played a predominant role at one moment or another? Is it possible, to paraphrase Saint Augustine, to 'see things as God sees them and not as human passions might wish them to be?'

Necessarily vague, the answers to these questions point towards a human vocation which becomes clear only in the light of progressive spiritual expansion.

When we obey the Law of Life, its dynamism and its rhythm, we fulfil our vocation, which is a vocation of intelligence. We become aware of the task required of us and of the discernment necessary for its accomplishment. We become aware of Primordial Liberty, which makes our choice possible. We understand that by giving free rein to our appetites, which nourish our greed, we are opening Pandora's box and helping to spread the scourges which it contains. We realize that the lust for power promotes fear and drives us to use unfair methods to dominate others, with the eventual result that conditions of conflict are created by our own actions.

We know that we must replace the lid on the famous box, but we do not understand that the effort is easier than it might seem, even though courage is certainly required.

In fact, we must dare to change course and to abandon personal beliefs so that we may approach the difficulties of existence and the problems of the world in another frame of mind.

An individual can achieve this transformation. Although it is composed of individuals, a society will certainly have greater difficulty.

When we consider the mission which the West is called upon to accept, we cannot avoid noting that in the past the West has failed to fulfil it.

Once it had conquered the world, the West should have implanted everywhere the humanism born on its soil, adapting it to local conditions and integrating it into the ancient traditions of the conquered regions. It sinned by omission, not in all times and places, but often. Subsequently, when it withdrew and abandoned its conquests, it suffered guilt, particularly because its retreat was a failure caused by its inability to prepare an élite to initiate or carry on a civilizing effort.

A guilty conscience resolves nothing, and the abdication of responsibility helps no one except those conspirators who usurp the unoccupied positions of leadership.

Wiser after two world wars, the West must get a grip on itself in order to preserve the essential elements of a civilization which contains many positive aspects.

Some may doubt it. Conflicts are legion, confrontations proliferate, ideologies oppose one another, cataclysms threaten, and the nuclear menace is growing, as are the number of nuclear warheads aimed at possible enemies. Fear prevails and is spreading. Since we have done everything and overlooked nothing to create such a situation, let us be confident that it can be improved if we act differently.

Let us face fear bravely, understanding that fear alone keeps Pandora's box open. Fear lies at the origin of all ills, intensifying them; this in turn increases fear, which then accentuates the problems anew. We should be able to interrupt this vicious circle. The first step is to acknowledge the existence of fear.

Fear was the very first feeling experienced by Adam and Eve after eating the fruit of the Tree of the Knowledge of Good and Evil. They were afraid that God would notice their disobedience. Seeing one another naked did nothing to reassure them, nor did the idea of experiencing death.

Once they had forsaken their state of unconsciousness and entered the world of duality and of time, Adam and

Eve were vulnerable to the threats of nature which had turned hostile. Their descendants, seeking to protect themselves against this threat, imagined an all-powerful Being and tried to maintain themselves in his good favour. Wishing to honour him, they built altars to false gods. They went to great lengths to impose their beliefs upon others in order to protect themselves – or so they thought – from unknown howling, burning, roaring forces which they hoped to master.

Religious wars followed. They never stopped.

It is human nature to worry, to wish to find an explanation for whatever is not understood. Human beings use expedients and create fictions to fill the void represented by the unknown. They shape these expedients to suit their desires, and worship them to gain confidence in their methods. This leads to ambition, the lust for power and competition in search of results.

Consequently, the slightest reversal of fortune provokes anxiety and doubt. These give rise to mental turmoil, which in turn increases anxiety. Fear and anxiety are not synonymous. We can be anxious without necessarily knowing why, whereas we are afraid of someone or something in particular.

When anxiety, fear and agitation fall prey to imagination, they produce illusion. Since illusions oppose one another, they lead to conflict, and since each of us is attached to his own illusion, the environment in which we exist becomes filled with confusion.

Failing to understand why we suffer, why we are here in this apparently absurd, frightening world, we develop theories and seek scapegoats.

None the less, anxiety and fear also serve a constructive function, forcing us to abandon all security in order constantly to renew the fruits of our experience.

The fear of fear itself produces a transformation. We

learn to let go, to cut our moorings in order to attain a different vision of our duties and responsibilities.

On the other hand, if fear is repressed, whatever form it takes can lead to avoidance. We give ourselves up to arbitrary notions, dedicate ourselves to violence, take refuge in drugs, rebel against the world or merely turn our back upon it, and wish for an Armageddon, hoping to perish in a great holocaust – but certainly not alone!

Trapped by earthly duality, forgetful of our original unity, we fall victim to our superstitions, fictions and illusions.

As a result, we experience anxiety and the conflict it produces. At this point we might ask: do superstitions, fictions, illusions and anxieties force us to turn inward in order to discover the reasons underlying these conflicts? Might our conflicts be due to the opposition between our two natures, one instinctive and rational, belonging to the creature which forms our ego, and the other, intuitive and inspired, belonging to the authentic Being?

Since the aspiration towards the Good, the True and the Beautiful, which is part of the realm of Being, is hampered by the desires and fears of the creature, we may wonder how to rid ourselves of these obstacles, how to eliminate the barriers which prevent us from transcending instinctive and mental forces.

The answer is easy: we must strip away whatever hinders us. However, it is not so simple to strip away the obstacles, since we must start by stripping away the opinion we have of ourselves and of the world. An effort of will is needed to abandon our opinions, since we must renounce all clichés, including those concerning good and evil. Then, free from all conditioning, we are aware each instant of the proper path of action.

All renunciation requires constant vigilance having as its sole object lucid availability. A clear understanding of the true causes of problems enables us to see them in the right perspective and thereby to discover appropriate solutions.

Availability leads to serenity and to correct thought, which in turn inspires correct action. If we are aware that even the complex alchemy of the body, and hence of all psychosomatic interactions, is dependent upon the mechanism of thought, then correct thought becomes an imperative which cannot be overemphasized.

Thinking correctly means taking into account all implications perceived at each instant, with no interference from the screen formed by desires, fears, passions or other impulses.

Free from all reactions, we can approach difficulties with the calmness of a mind at rest. This makes it possible, not to be more intelligent than before, but to be intelligent *with all our intelligence*.

Mental confusion creates illusion. When each person is attached to his own illusion, a chaotic state results; however, this state has the potential of leading to a beneficial reversal.

The fear of nuclear war, the pollution of the air, the degradation of nature, the extinction of certain animal species, and the death of the oceans can lead to an understanding of our human vocation, which is to collaborate in full awareness with the Great Work of Nature.

The terrestrial experience pursues its course, permitting us as travellers to become aware of the reasons behind this living experience and to understand that our present fears, as well as those we may have in the future, must be forgotten if we are to develop the hope implicit in our predestination.

Calm and serene, we can then discover what is immutable behind constant mobility; in other words, we can discover Supreme Order which governs the manifestation of the Truths of Life.

Thus the particles of the atom are arranged in minuscule solar systems; the curvature of a tangerine illustrates a logic immanent in the physical world; and in the act of picking a flower, we touch the stars.

Everything is contained within everything else and the interdependence of multiple energy fields links the smallest electron to the entire universe, and the universe to the electron.

From this perspective, personal problems lose their magnitude. By integrating them into a vaster framework, we discover the superior design of Life which is an integral part of evolution based upon experience. We understand that although Intelligence always triumphs eventually, on an individual level such intelligence requires self-knowledge. Only self-knowledge frees the reason from accumulated sediment bringing about the indispensable adherence of intelligence to one's decisions. Thus one is convinced that whatever is intuitively perceived corresponds to the truth of the moment.

Such a conviction, based upon the union of reason and intuition, serves as a guiding light for the explorer, orienting the scientist as well as the individual who seeks Truth.

'Stand up and walk', command the Scriptures, and the free human being can in fact raise his head toward Heaven while keeping his feet firmly planted on the ground.

He can dream without giving himself up to these dreams, which are transformed into a living reality by myths, symbols and legends. Do these not in fact correspond to the age-old longing for a supernatural world?

The proud heirs of the Greek miracle are responsible for discerning the value that the Hellenic sages attributed to myths and legends, which transmit an ever-living symbolism intended to inform human beings and to allow them, through their understanding of the messages, to escape the constraints imposed by the imponderable elements manifesting themselves between heaven and earth.

The symbolism suggests that a proper sense of proportion should prevail in the search for harmony. As the guiding principle of love, harmony leads to Cognizance which reveals the right solution through a perfect adaptation to the circumstances of the moment.

Greek mythology transmits a rich symbolism of psychological teachings, ranging from the exploits of Theseus to the tragic destiny of Oedipus, from the triumph of Bellerophon over Chimera to the immolation of the children of Jason, a pure hero perverted by the charms of the beautiful sorceress Medea and her stunning powers.

In the background of myth, tragedy or legend can be discerned the inspiration of the gods which has become accessible to man. Man's intelligence must serve as a balance between opposing forces within him so that the scale hovers permanently near its centre of stability.

Otherwise, driven by the anxiety of our intellect and besieged by our emotions, we lose our way and our enterprises deteriorate.

Failure upon failure causes us to react, and we then choose the so-called left-hand path of hate, fanaticism and lust for power in order to escape – or so we think – from an apparently blind, and therefore undeserved, destiny.

A foolhardy undertaking, and one to be avoided!

CHAPTER 7

Are We Civilized?

The mission of the West is to transmit a civilization which humanity cannot repudiate without harm.

Consequently, it is essential to ask what civilization is. How can we define this term which, from north to south and from east to west, changes content and meaning?

We must also not forget that the term 'abdication' mentioned earlier suggests decadence. The causes of this decadence merit attention. Since too many factors can lead to misunderstanding, we must approach these fundamental considerations with lucidity and extreme caution before drawing conclusions. Our thoughtless habit of using ready-made definitions causes us to accept them uncritically. To convince ourselves of this fact, we need only examine the image which comes to mind when we think of a civilized person.

Do we imagine someone who knows how to move gracefully in social, political, professional or family circles of a particular period? Do we imagine someone effortlessly handling all kinds of technologies, or perhaps someone with refined taste using each object with elegance – in other words someone who is cultured and has useful knowledge?

The list could be lengthened if we chose to emphasize

the attractive aspects of the term 'civilized'. Unfortunately, these attractive aspects do not correspond to the
harsh realities of the moment nor to the spectacle provided by the so-called civilized world.

This spectacle is one of decadence, accelerated by lust
and reinforced by a 'consumer society' and its excessive
taste for pleasure, skilfully maintained by psychological
methods employed at different levels.

These methods urge us to demand our rights while
forgetting our duties. They push us into the race for
material possessions which proliferate thanks to our
ingenuity. The constant appeal to greed produces the
fear of being in want and sharpens excessive appetites.
Violence spreads – cynical, sly, remote-controlled.

We not only prey upon one another, but we are ill with
a contagious disease.

Are we civilized?

All excesses undermine civilization, which should be
an expression of the relationships linking us to the
universe and therefore to Supreme Order.

The means available to us, which have been increased
by science and technology, should not arouse our cruelty
nor sustain our drive for power. On the contrary, they
should serve humanity, which is destined in its particular
domain to manifest harmony as a path to happiness. That
is the reason for the place occupied by civilization in the
evolutionary spiral, and the experience of missed oppor-
tunities ought to make Western man aware of this fact.

The adjective 'civilized' does not seem appropriate to
Western man, although in many parts of the world,
people are awakening, great works are being accomplished, political systems are being established and social
theories are being developed, all with the idea of
adapting technologies, knowledge and ways of life to
Western standards.

Envied and reviled, Western man must be able to distinguish the high from the low points of his evolution, in order to discover in its winding path his human vocation, identical to the vocation of the community to which he belongs.

Since our civilization is technological, the problems of modern man must be placed in a scientific and technological context, and it is only in relation to daily reality that solutions for attaining well-being can be considered.

The attainment of well-being is the goal of the so-called philosopical path leading to an art of living which produces happiness. Although 'existing well' provides indisputable satisfactions, these are likely to be only temporary. On the other hand, happiness is a state which can be attained. Those who reach it experience an inexhaustible joy which they seek to preserve by avoiding everything which might endanger it.

If well-being is to be attained, a fundamental revolution is essential. Only by means of such a revolution can a political, social, economic and technological order be established which will be different from bureaucratic organization based upon the abdication of personal initiative and the unconditional submission of the individual. In return for his submission, such organization offers a material security more apparent than real, since in this world of permanent economic upheaval, pensions, annuities or other promised benefits are at the very best uncertain.

If we contemplate Western civilization as it appears to an impartial observer, we may discover the profound reasons underlying the convulsions and their disastrous consequences, which are quite obvious.

We may be able to discover solutions which strike at the roots of the problem rather than at its effects. As already stated, these roots can be traced to fear in all its forms. Moreover, isolation resulting from broken family bonds increases the disarray caused by fear. It is no exaggeration to say that ignorance of the reasons for human suffering lies at the origin of the conflicts which produce fear – conflicts which fear, giving bad counsel, perpetuates.

Let us be aware of the facts, not in order to establish social, political, economic or philosophical theories, but rather in order to transcend them all. Since progress, prosperity, efficiency and profitability have not kept their miraculous promises, today more than ever we must visualize the foundations of a true civilization upon which to build the world of tomorrow.

We have learned how to master extremely powerful energies. We construct robots – mechanical marvels which can completely change our way of work, freeing us from tasks that they can accomplish better than we.

The conquests of science constantly push back the frontiers of the unknown. Matter dissolves into a vortex of energies, and it is said that a particular curvature of the space–time continuum creates particles, the elementary building blocks of our universe.

Radar scans space; radio probes explore distant planets; information is instantaneous and, retransmitted by satellites, is immediately accessible on television screens.

The sky belongs to man, and planes fly several times faster than the speed of sound. Basic research is progressing and, according to predictions, biological discoveries may make it possible to create conditions favourable to the emergence of life.

It should be emphasized that only the conditions favourable to the emergence of life can be created, since life 'is' without beginning or end, and no one is able to create the unknowable.

Everything existing reflects life, and although the forms it animates disappear and reappear, no one has ever perceived it. Man, almost a demigod, revels in his power, but he also fears that the forces he has unleashed may destroy him.

Although the spectre of nuclear war haunts him, nuclear weapons still proliferate. The phantom of galloping demography and of ensuing hunger threaten certain parts of the globe, but such facts fail to stop the squandering of wealth and the spread of wastelands produced by the frenzied exploitation of the earth's surface.

The pollution of oceans and waterways is destroying the habitat of animal species, which are consequently disappearing, threatening the human environment as well. Man loudly proclaims these threats and yet continues wasting the earth's bounty, discounting pleas for caution. Such caution conflicts with his greed, and the very fact that nuclear, biological or bacteriological warfare can be envisaged illustrates his confusion and inner turmoil.

In fact, every war is only the projection of our inner conflict multiplied by that of others. The monstrous threat of cosmic destruction looms on the horizon and we in the West, having made this possible, now have the responsibility to avert it.

Carried away by a sort of delirium resulting from our pride, our lust for power and our anxiety, we have finally reached the point of envisaging an Armageddon. The fact that prophecies of doom are becoming increasingly detailed and numerous exacerbates our anxiety.

Our contradictions support the conviction that we are helpless victims of fate. We refuse to admit that we are the artisans of our destiny, preferring to blame chance, a convenient word masking our lack of wisdom.

Although we want to believe that the worst can be

avoided, we fail to realize that the violation of our own nature leads to a repression of our essential aspirations. Wishing to distract ourselves, we mistake agitation for entertainment and are thereby diverted from the essential.

Our powers can be creative or destructive and, guided by our will, utilizing the gifts developed by appropriate exercises, we are capable of using psychic powers to influence others. We know how to use key words to inflame a crowd. We create slogans to demolish our real or potential adversaries. We enjoy our dominance, which makes us forget the anguish we feel when we are alone with ourselves, forced to acknowledge the void within.

Driven by the poison of constant sensationalism, we feel lost in a world of accelerated transformation. We would like to understand, but we do not know how to listen. Incapable of dissolving the barrier of resistance formed by our psychological, religious, scientific or spiritual prejudices, we try to listen from behind this barrier, and what we hear is actually only our own noise.

There is an art to listening, but a calm mind is required to attune to the speaker in order to hear him, not only with our ears, but with our intuition.

These are critical times. If the catastrophes so widely predicted are to be avoided, we must rediscover true wisdom, which will make it possible to overcome the obstacles periodically blocking humanity's path.

It is absurd to curse science and technology; these reflect the creative genius of humanity. However, to bend them to our own law instead of submitting them to The Law may entail destruction.

Only awakened Intelligence derived from a genuine understanding, and thereby stripped of the veils woven by ignorance, will allow the new age to flourish and to spread the justice of the gods.

Although ignorance is indeed the enemy to be defeated, it is not enough merely to assert this fact.

We may know things without understanding the essential, which is to foster an awakening and therefore another state of consciousness. Such a state is not attained in the same way as we learn a lesson. We must dissolve anything preventing us from stepping over the threshold beyond which everything changes. If we are to facilitate this crossing, we must return to our sources.

CHAPTER 8

The Truth of the Moment

Any generalization involves, by definition, elements of error, since at best the events of a particular period can merely illustrate a tendency, producing effects which vary according to time and place.

However, one thing is certain. A salient feature of rapid technological change is the substitution of artificial products for natural ones. Such change produces a physiological transformation with yet unforeseen consequences which are only gradually appearing. Since these affect our psychological universe, they undoubtedly also have an effect upon our behaviour. Mental effort today is yielding to the electronic calculator. Free choice is being voluntarily limited and subordinated to information provided by computers which have gained predominance in businesses as well as in the governmental ministries responsible for war and peace.

The chemical components of food modify the complex alchemy of the body. The use of artificial fertilizers in agriculture and the use of hormones for livestock also produce biological reactions in the human being.

Markets are invaded by frozen, dehydrated and freeze-dried food. Synthetic fibres replace wool. Tenderizers used for meats destroy their nutritive value.

The heat employed in cooking is replaced by a micro-wave process which dissociates the molecules in food to make consumption possible.

The pill modifies the biological rhythm of women, and genetics provides the means to manufacture supermen or perhaps monsters.

It is taken for granted that we will be able to create conditions necessary for the development of life. In our pride, we may exclaim that we have created it, unaware that life cannot be created, but 'is' for all eternity.

In our ignorance of the Laws of Life we advocate abortion, not caring that when the energetic particle called a soul is expelled from its natural habitat, it may take refuge in another womb. Malformations may result if there is dissonance between its own particular rhythm and that of the woman sheltering it, or between its own ethnic heritage and the woman's, whose evolution may not correspond to its own. Consequently, one day rebellion breaks out and hate boils over.

Do we realize that in only one decade abortions have claimed more lives in the West than the horrors of two world wars?

Despite the fact that research continues and a succession of inventions sustains the belief in progress, we might understandably wonder whether human advancement is actually taking place.

Left to himself, modern man becomes bored. He turns on the radio or the television. Even at work, he needs background noise. He walks through the streets, plugging his ears with headsets from portable transistors. Children, accustomed to sophisticated toys, no longer know how to play. City-dwellers, feeling disoriented, consult mediums, astrologers or psychiatrists. They have no ideal to sustain them in their daily preoccupations.

Disenchanted, they jump headlong into futile

adventures, hoping to find in the euphoria of drugs, in terrorism, in fanaticism, or in constant diversion an outlet to their longing for an undefined 'somewhere else'.

Does artificiality dehumanize its willing victims, or in the long run, does it help them to master a misunderstood destiny? In the latter case, how can such mastery be achieved? These fundamental questions lead us to the problem of the vocation of Western man and, consequently, to the mission of the West itself.

Although still nebulous, and despite the fact that all sorts of excesses seem to favour decline, awareness is dawning in the West, as illustrated for example by the increasingly widespread search for a master. This search is a sign of youth in rebellion who seek understanding rather than mere belief. However, the younger generation willingly imagines that it can only find far away from home the exceptional being capable of guiding its quest.

The desire to find such a being threatens to lead this quest along a false path. Imagining what a master might be, we may encounter him without recognizing him. We do not want to go wrong, but still we may fall victim to illusion.

It is too easy to forget that a master never boasts of his virtues or his powers, that he avoids exerting the least influence, and that he abstains from statements capable of arousing satisfaction at the idea of being a privileged pupil.

None the less, the search for a master is the symptom of an essential aspiration, which is to discover how to fulfil our destiny.

In fact, our century is profoundly religious despite appearances to the contrary. Although on the one hand seminaries and monasteries are emptying, on the other,

Zen, Tibetan and similar centres are attracting large numbers of adepts. Groups are forming, communities are springing up, and sects are multiplying, promising members a different kind of existence.

The good and bad are intermingled, and the exploitation of essential aspirations is at its height.

Even so, the trend is spreading, and the search for Truth is touching increasingly broad segments of the population.

What is this Truth which so many wish to find? It seems elusive, since some seek it while others claim to possess it and still others declare: 'To each his own!'

Despite the obvious fact that Truth cannot be categorized, it is important to try and clarify the subject. Truth corresponds to the vision of the moment, but this instant of Truth illuminates the entire being. It does not enclose us in a false certainty of having found truth once and for all.

Truth participates in the rhythm of life and can only be grasped beyond the movement of forms, which reveal its innumerable facets. Truth merges with the reality behind appearances, and this reality is itself linked to different levels of perception, which extend from the physical plane to the supramental or spiritual one.

For some, truth is what is observable; for others it corresponds to a divine ideation expressed by the Word. What is observable is situated within the double polarity of this world. Daily experience makes duality perceptible; it is a fact on the existential plane. On the other hand, divine ideation corresponds to universal law – the Logos of the ancients – and this reality transcends polarity, being situated beyond yin and yang, beyond the active and the passive, beyond the masculine and the feminine.

Between the two extremes of what is observable and

what is sacred lies the occult world. We have for too long and too stubbornly denied miracles and are therefore surprised at the current interest in parapsychology, alternative medicine and spiritualism.

'There is nothing hidden which shall not be revealed.' None the less, there is a danger in the attraction of the occult. In order to penetrate the arcana of an invisible universe, preparation is necessary. We must not desire to find there what we are seeking, nor should we imagine that familiar notions apply.

To approach the occult world with preconceived ideas is the most certain way to accept interpretations which are at best only partially valid and more probably entirely false.

We must go beyond all mental projections in order to understand, rather than believe in, something which cannot be verified.

In one of the apocryphal gospels, it is said: 'When the feminine is no longer feminine and the masculine is no longer masculine, you will enter the Kingdom.' This statement, attributed to Jesus, leads us back to the problem of existential duality.

Let us turn our attention briefly to Calvary. Although the term 'apocryphal' has come to mean 'doubtful', its original meaning referred to a secret. Beyond the human drama, might the crucifixion have concealed a secret? Calvary offers us the tragic spectacle of Jesus crucified between two thieves – a powerful image rich in teachings. Why was Jesus crucified between two thieves who opposed one another in their last moments? One of them awakens to life eternal whereas the other, irreversibly blind, addresses some cruel words to the sublime messenger.

Every symbol transmits an essential idea. Might the poignant drama of Calvary be a symbol? Might it not represent man, tortured between good and evil, being born to life through death?

Might we not conclude that life, always triumphant, pursues its living adventure even if existence and its duality are suspended?

On the existential level, good and evil are opposites. Evil prevails when we seek power for our own gain or for the benefit of the systems with which we identify ourselves.

On the other hand, good is that which assures harmony of body and mind and overcomes the turmoil of passions.

Opposition is a source of perpetual confusion and therefore of conflict. 'I am torn between the evil that I do and the good that I wish to do', exclaimed Ovid, as well as many others before and after him.

The individual who is greedy for earthly pleasures, for emotions, knowledge and intellectual vanities, creates fear, which is the root of conflict.

Humanity is tormented by fear of the unknown, and science, as it pushes back the limits of the known, magnifies such fear by revealing an increasing complexity in the universe. The interplay of opposites seduces us into straying from the path of Truth, which is also the path leading to the Tree of Life in the centre of the Garden of Eden.

Since they have eaten the fruit of the Tree of the Knowledge of Good and Evil, human beings, forgetful of their original unity, succumb to the illusion of the duality of existence.

They try to find the path which leads to the Tree of Life, but good intentions do not suffice. The road to hell is paved with good intentions, which human beings invoke to cloak their desires, passions and vices.

Victims of duality, we are in constant conflict with

ourselves. When we yield to this conflict we are not free, and therefore we are incapable of reaching a state of harmony which transcends forces in opposition to one another.

To attain harmony is to achieve a perfect balance of the three aspects of our constitution – physical, psychological and spiritual; it is to allow our true nature to blossom.

Using tricks, clever ruses and pseudo-spiritual attitudes, enthralled by captivating theories and doctrines which lure our intellect, we become attached to temporal satisfactions, imagining ourselves capable of serving God and Mammon at the same time.

'He who walks in darkness does not know where he is going', Saint John said. Indeed, lack of discernment causes us to walk in the shadows of the unconscious which contain, none the less, the buried memories of all past experiences. 'We may discover the world without leaving our chair,' said a sage of the past, 'because the world is within each of us.' 'A drop of water in the sea', he continues, 'knows perhaps that it belongs to the sea, but it may be unaware that the sea is within it as well.'

God and the devil are within us, but it is mostly the devil who creates a great uproar. He is a supreme master in the art of attracting attention. Scandals, murders, conflicts, controversies and other disturbances fill the front pages of our newspapers.

We might have the impression that the devil is leading a gigantic dance. This is true to the extent that, carried away in a diabolical frenzy, we seek fleeting success and try to bend nature to our own law. Defeats follow upon victories and victories upon defeats, yet we refuse to give up our foolish dreams.

The strength of our genius leaves its mark upon the world: we graft trees; we create new species and we modify the earth's appearance. Satisfaction dwells in our heart, which is abandoned by happiness and invaded by anxiety.

We might recall that the Tree of Life is guarded by angels and that immortality is distilled in our own body when we allow our soul to vibrate like a harp in unison with the Soul of the World – in other words, when we harmonize our essential rhythm with the pure rhythm of spirit.

When we ourselves have become angelic, we will be able to approach the Tree of Life in the Garden of Eden, pick the golden fruits in the Garden of the Hesperides and ascend into the radiant ether where the immortals dwell.

This metaphor is part of the 'Golden Verses' attributed to Pythagoras, who saw in the realized human being a potential god. The Bible seems to confirm this.

The Bible speaks of an apprentice god who in all logic should be able to attain mastery, provided he becomes aware of his tools, provided he understands the Great Work which requires his collaboration, provided he is available in his heart and soul.

CHAPTER 9

The Challenge

Sooner or later every mission provokes challenges. The challenge which the West must face is both external and internal. These two aspects are linked to its scientific, technological and psychological development, and to discoveries which have upset ideas which until recently were firmly established.

Before considering how these challenges manifest themselves and before deciding how to meet them, let us reflect upon how modern science, wrongly accused of being responsible for the ills of society, is transforming our vision of the universe.

'Don't make me laugh,' exclaimed Heisenberg, a Nobel prize-winning physicist and undoubtedly one of the best known atomic scientists of our times. 'You talk about electrons and waves. Have you seen them? Do you think you can observe a nucleus, an electron or a wave? Forget it! You will never see them. The wave which carries an electron is nothing more than a wave of probability.'

Might our world be governed by probability? If so, why do we so obstinately seek the reassurance of certainty, which is apparently contrary to the Laws of Nature? Nature turns, bends and pulls once again into its design anything opposed to it, and Wisdom therefore requires a constant adaptation to ever-shifting conditions.

To be open-minded at each instant, free from all concepts, available and aware of whatever presents itself, not only increases our understanding, but also makes possible a judicious choice appropriate to all circumstances.

Although science has managed to dissect the atom, it has not solved the mystery of our origins. The reasons for our terrestrial journey remain unknown. 'Where do we come from? Where are we going?' are eternal questions for humanity.

Delving into the infinitely small universe of atoms and particles, we are perplexed, no longer knowing whether what we observe is the ultimate structure of matter or a whirling energy which escapes our observation.

Everything moves, shifts and changes: galaxies, the solar system, the planets, earth, atoms and particles.

Uncertainty, elevated to the level of a physical law, perhaps reflects a cosmic reality which invites the awakened human being, witness and actor on the world's stage, to admit that constant transformation requires him to abandon an outdated routine which limits his possibilities.

Nature protects those who are faithful to her programme, a programme which varies according to species. Because we fail to heed the movement of rhythm, we are the victims of an inertia which is part of nature. Our actions are contrary to the Laws of Nature, and in our frustration we ask science to provide us with the reassurance of security.

Science cannot satisfy us, since it cannot integrate into its formulas our secret aspirations and our nostalgia for a marvellous place elsewhere.

This utopia, which even the imagination cannot conceive, belongs to the sphere of metaphysics, which encompasses the vast realm beyond the sensory universe. However,, with great reluctance modern science is incorporating metaphysics into its domain.

Sophisticated instruments – electronic microscopes, cyclotrons, computers – can lead the aware person towards a comprehension transcending the senses. A different dimension can be discovered beneath technological achievements, which dazzle those who created them.

The fundamental unity of the universe can be perceived by means of experiments pursued in the most diverse fields. This unity, sensed before being proved, cannot be described, since conventional language is inadequate to the task.

Perhaps our brain transforms reality, which manifests itself through successive rhythmic impulses, into objects, events, colours or sounds. The universe as we perceive it exists solely in our consciousness and only the mystic, escaping for a mere instant from the mental boundaries which condition him, can harmonize the rhythm of his soul with the rhythm of the cosmos. The instant of truth which the mystic thereby experiences illuminates his entire being, since he merges for a brief instant with the incommensurable awareness of an unthinkable reality.

Einstein was persuaded of this when he stated: 'The most beautiful and profound emotion which we can experience is a mystical sensation. It is the seed of all true science. The person to whom this emotion is unknown, who is no longer capable of surprise or wonder, seems as if he were dead.'

Therefore, let us be alive, inspired by wonder, and let us think correctly, realizing that thought determines not only the physiology of our bodies, but also the vital dynamism which circulates in our nervous system.

The world is our laboratory. Let us not transform it into a purgatory by opposing the Laws of Life. Let us realize that the extreme variety of spiritual, cultural, political, social, chemical, biological and physical combinations are, through their interactions, the kaleidoscopic mirror of a supraphysical reality which reveals itself as an inherent logic in the manifest universe.

Such a view is opposed to a widely advocated philosophy which claims that the West is decadent, a mere corpse awaiting decomposition.

A society, and indeed every human group, develops according to laws which are not very different from those discovered by the scientist in his basic research.

The atomic scientist knows that when a critical threshold is crossed, a sudden transformation occurs which can be likened to a brutal explosion. In the West, this critical threshold may be attained relatively soon. A single drop of water could then cause the cup to overflow. Great efforts must be made to avoid such a situation, since the explosion threatens to be particularly painful.

The danger is increased in a mechanized world by information fed to us from every direction, by the heavy pressure of bureaucratic organizations and by ecological deterioration.

Only lucid perception can lead to constructive solutions. It is an illusion to imagine that the cessation of scientific research might resolve the problems of our times. To reject science would be to turn our back on an evolutionary reality which is an integral part of the Order of Things.

On the other hand, human progress can be served by scientific thought, which requires a constant re-evaluation of everything which once seemed certain. To be receptive to the world in the same way that a scientist is receptive to an experiment, without prior assumptions, is an attitude which we would be wise to imitate.

'As above, so below', states the Emerald Tablet, the origins of which are attributed to Hermes Trismegistus, the metaphysical god of the Egyptians. Why not accept the teachings of an ancient wisdom and act accordingly? What is right on one level is also right on another.

The constant adaptation of our actions to the realities of the moment is the opposite of a passive attitude which lazily accepts falsehoods stated and repeated with great assurance. If we deliberately mislead those whom we seek to convince or seduce, we are making them pervious to all kinds of influences and may create hate and conflict.

Modern scientific thought, which erases the demarcation line between the visible and invisible worlds of physics and metaphysics, is part of a process of unification. It helps us realize that the separation of diverse discipline – chemistry, biology, sociology, psychology and others – is obsolete. Such a realization leads to a vision of ultimate unification, not only of the different levels of human activity, but also of different spiritual or religious traditions, since the One Truth affirms its unity while pursuing its living adventure in the diversity of forms it adopts.

Any discussion of science today brings to mind nuclear weapons. Their development simply illustrates the misunderstanding of the true predestination of man, whose creative genius has gone astray in the search for power rather than for happiness.

A scientific understanding of the laws of the ambient world leads to a discovery of a Supreme Order, to a discovery that such Supreme Order reigns within us and that humanity, intimately linked to the universe, exists only through this Order.

Consequently, when we study nature we are studying man; when we oppose the Laws of Nature we are opposing ourselves; when we destroy nature we are destroying humanity.

On the other hand, every action which is attuned to the order of the cosmic plan creates harmony and, therefore, joy and happiness.

Modern science can be the spearhead of a true Renaissance, provided it is used wisely and is integrated into the cosmic plan of evolution, which tends to carry everything towards final perfection.

'Whoever does not waste his allotted time on earth is in no danger', Pythagoras has said. 'His own light will show the way.'

Our apprenticeship should allow us to 'recognize error and see Truth', so that we may realize that existential realities become infused with beauty when they are ennobled by a high level of consciousness, and that daily life is a field of experience leading to the discovery of the 'Self'.

'Whoever truly loves knowledge seeks to attain the Self', Plato said.

It is only in the transparency of its nature that the authentic innermost Being can manifest itself. The attainment of this transparency is the final stage of alchemical transformation, of essential self-realization.

Self-realization does not mean the replacement of obsolete notions by others, but a gradual broadening of our vision, in the manner of a mountain climber whose view expands as he ascends to discover new, ever-larger vistas beyond the opaque walls of rock which enclose him.

At the summit is revealed the 'limitless', bathed in the light of the sun – not just a physical star, but also the pure mirror of the Cosmic Spirit.

CHAPTER 10

Paradox Reigns Supreme!

If we are to understand the dual nature of the challenge facing the West, we must clarify the reasons behind it.

Let us abstain from any judgement, condemnation or approval, since our sole purpose is to discover the roots of the perils which, if they persist, may provoke a planetary conflict.

Therefore, we must be impartial witnesses, free from passion, emotion or reaction. We must discard all opinions or intellectual concepts based upon superficial observations or upon clichés resulting from accumulated errors which we accept without bothering to verify their accuracy.

Only in a state of awareness and comprehension can we see the world as it is; only when we are free from obsolete notions can we understand without prejudice. Such a state of awareness entails the use of clear and precise words to avoid any distortion of meaning and requires a continuous adjustment to shifting conditions – in other words, a constantly renewed awareness of each instant.

Then, beyond family or national ties, beyond the notion of time which limits perception, we may discover the visible and invisible relationships which provide a clear vision of the world as it is now and which offer the means to solve problems in full awareness of the supreme order.

Anything which contradicts this order creates confusion and disarray. Let us be aware that the squandering of goods by rich nations, the exhaustion of non-renewable resources, ecological pollution, the demographic explosion, the ravages of hunger as well as more localized conflicts are mere attendant phenomena which contribute to the general confusion.

A psychological revolution is of paramount importance in helping science rediscover its proper role and in helping us find very different remedies from those adopted through habit and conservatism despite repeated failures.

The revolt of youth, who turn their backs upon a society – to which they belong, however – is a distinctive feature of the transformation which is now in its early stages.

Even if excesses have been committed by certain extreme elements of this revolt, it may be helpful to examine the motives of those involved in order to discover some potentially useful ideas behind the apparent rebellion.

One characteristic of some of today's youth is a disdain for success and money. This disdain is in fact ambivalent. On the one hand, young people apparently no longer believe in the value of work, since they ridicule success, yet on the other they boast of being ready to wreck society in order to purify the world and create an industrious and honest community.

Paradox reigns supreme. Some wish to elevate decadence to the level of an art, thereby creating a counterculture. Others jump into terrorism, ready to die for an elevated ideal.

The desire to satisfy personal needs is considered sufficient justification for petty thievery, although those committing such acts may claim not to have any such needs; others may oppose the established social order out of bravado, wishing in fact to find human warmth and a reason for existence. The comradeship of complicity is highly valued, filling the void created by broken family ties. These are replaced by groups formed around brief common ventures.

Drugs are taken to relieve boredom, to fulfil a desire to be like others, or to escape the hidden anxiety created by the belief in one's uselessness.

Society is indeed facing a collective crisis of consciousness resulting from the progressive disintegration of common values. The profit motive, rational logic and efficiency are among the accused.

Although sociologists and educators have examined the problem of youth, they have failed to find effective remedies to what might be called our contemporary malaise.

Today, this malaise assumes particular importance, since our means of self-destruction are more powerful than ever. Moreover, never before has vice produced such a level of exploitation.

To fulfil its vocation, the West must first undertake a deep self-examination in order to discover its soul, veiled by so many apparent contradictions. This self-examination cannot occur without an effort to discover the profound reasons behind the revolt of the young, and the not-so-young, against a society to which they belong.

The dream of a new age is not a sufficient explanation.

Let us examine the facts.

Our modern world is in a generally observable pathological state, manifesting a neurosis which has become increasingly all-pervasive. The consumption of large amounts of barbiturates and other chemicals by the population proves the accuracy of this observation, and recent events, which indicate an increasing tendency towards barbarism, sadism and a total disregard for human life, are making it even more clear.

Humanity seems eager to degrade itself, and since experience proves that causes can be discovered even among the least apparent symptoms, we will not content ourselves with the mere repetition of general formulas.

'For want of an idea, a new word is invented to replace it!' Goethe said. Let us avoid this trap!

The question is too important to be examined only superficially. Although the effects may be known, the causes are more difficult to discern, since an apparent cause may actually be an effect which had escaped previous observation or had been wrongly interpreted.

Without dwelling upon it, let us heed what is said by many of those who are eager to find a quick explanation of the facts. We may discover that they draw diametrically opposed conclusions based upon arguments which they consider irrefutable.

They may say: 'Our society needs to be razed to the ground, since its structures are out of date.' Or they may say: 'Our society of production and consumption is absurd.' Or: 'We must abolish profit; we must return to nature, to the horse and carriage, to oil lamps.'

Little is said, however, about man: what he is, why he is, where he comes from and where he is going.

On the other hand, many intellectually attractive proposals are suggested, pure mental creations devoid of any comprehension of physical and spiritual realities.

The word 'civilization' does not merely refer to the creation and use of technology. It also includes the recognition of humanism as a complete expression of man. If civilization does in fact represent the complete expression of man, then today either civilization exists or it does not exist, but it is meaningless to speak, as many do, about a 'crisis of civilization'.

Civilization can be nothing else than the sum of civilized human beings. A person is civilized when he acts correctly and of his own accord with respect to whatever must be done at a particular moment, without constraint of law, and when he does so wherever fate places him.

His quality of heart and soul makes him the equal of every other human being and he reveals this quality while accomplishing his duty in full awareness of his human dignity.

Whether an intellectual or a manual labourer, whether rich or poor, he 'is'.

Can we say that such a person exists?

In order to 'Be', the wise person of whatever age must have the courage to jettison false notions, acquired habits and self-indulgent vices.

Whether young or old, everyone has preconceived opinions which should be discarded. In his time, Descartes noted that 'it is not as easy for a person to rid himself of his prejudices as it is for him to burn his house.'

Every prejudice obscures common sense, which no amount of knowledge can supplant. Indeed, badly assimilated knowledge often leads us astray.

Cartesian culture is often wrongly interpreted. We have not understood that Cartesianism requires each person to liberate his mind as completely as possible from everything which it has not carefully verified as perfectly acceptable to reason.

Cartesianism is the search for the authentic individual beneath the one conditioned by conventional behaviour, by codified and structured doctrines, and by habits. Sometimes, a young person is more conditioned than a middle-aged one, since in the course of his life the latter has had to abandon his errors fairly often. However, we may note that a certain psychological laziness can hamper the awareness necessary for mental freedom.

Psychological laziness is opposed to the normal evolution of living things. In a river, we never bathe in the same water twice. 'Everything passes', said Heraclitus.

However, the awakened individual recognizes his equal in another. Awakening requires the revival of essential values and their hierarchy – a term deriving from 'hieros', meaning 'sacred'.

It is therefore an error to think that we must create new values. In their essence, values are eternal and universal. However, changes can be wrought in the manifestation of what is eternal.

A hierarchy of values can be symbolized by a pyramid, which may be regarded as an image for a cosmo-biological structure inviting the adept, who has learned its secrets, to attempt an ascent. The ascent progresses from the square of the pyramid's base to the tip, which represents the Omega point, and illustrates the path leading from the limitations of existence to the limitlessness of Life which transcends it.

Once this is understood, we may return to our discussion of a hierarchy of values and note that such a hierarchy may be compared to a pyramid complete with its top, and not to a truncated one. We live in a world of superficial, incomplete notions, failing to realize that at each level of human evolution, our psychological and spiritual development must be taken into account.

When emphasizing the importance of new social or political structures or stressing the imperative necessity for greater social justice, which is obvious, we must understand what we really mean.

Just as the body is composed of cells which give it form

and consistency, so a society is composed of customs, a way of life and the quality of the individuals within it. The wish to change society because of its faults only has meaning if we recognize the necessity of rediscovering man in his totality. In order to give him a foundation for his evolution, adaptable structures are required.

We may prefer the prison of rigid structures because we lack the courage to change. Change is contrary to the principle of inertia which characterizes human nature.

Human beings, who would like to be the creators of perfect civilizations and ideal societies, are devoured by ambition, envy and egotism. Are we able to create something other than a projection of what we are? Are we, in all simplicity, aware of our own contradictions?

We rebel against society which crushes us by its means of production and consumption, but we still want to enjoy the advantages of technology. Therefore we claim our rights, without realizing that every claim for rights must be balanced by the recognition of duties.

The more humanity wants rights, the more necessary it becomes to fulfil these duties. Rights only exist when duties are accepted and effectively accomplished.

But if we consider the fulfilment of duties to be a burden, let us have the honesty to admit that it is because of our own constantly expanding demands.

The greater our greed, then the more demanding we become, the more we enslave ourselves, and the more we will be required to pay the tribute of suffering for our failure to understand that we alone are responsible for the world we criticize.

We attack our governments, condemning their inability to solve our difficulties. We hold them responsible for the turmoil and for the wars which are breaking out almost continuously. We wonder what to think of these events and we imagine solutions for the conflicts but, since we fail to adopt them, in reality all we are doing is condemning ourselves.

Therefore, if we consider that everyone should take an active part in the proper functioning of society, in its harmonious development, then everyone has the obligation to accept his responsibility wherever he finds himself and whatever his place. Each of us without exception is responsible for what we do, or for what we are called upon to do, wherever fate may summon us.

To be aware of our responsibility is to be aware of our human qualities, aware of our dignity, aware and proud of our participation in the common endeavour, proud also of fulfilling our duties before claiming our rights.

Such considerations bring to mind the problem of youth. We forget all too easily that although youth is a temporary state, we can remain young at all ages.

In Greece, a male child was entrusted to the care of the mother until the age of seven years. Then the father took over and taught him everything which might be useful to him, such as how to hold a plough or drive a chariot, as well as the significance of the proper measure for all things, so that he might live in harmony with the world, with humanity and with the gods.

In the days when chivalry flourished, the father would lead his adolescent son into combat. He taught him everything practical which he might need to know and everything which constituted the ideal of the period. As soon as the son had proved his prowess, he was armed as a knight. There was always a bond of continuity in spirit. The young knight had the correct sense of his dignity and of his noble quality of heart – noble in the best sense of the word.

Undoubtedly, this idealized image does not reflect the reality of the period. However, it does succeed in conveying the idea of a fundamental aspiration which is cruelly lacking today.

At present an enormous gap exists between the generations. The bond between them has not been broken, since it cannot be, but it is greatly strained.

Parents on the one hand, and society which has discovered the purchasing power of youth on the other, have created this gap. Parents have neglected their duties in their efforts to assure themselves a comfortable existence. Mothers work outside the home; fathers seek tranquillity; couples separate quickly, indulging many of their children's whims. Is it not regrettable that youngsters under fifteen years of age watch television for as many hours as they spend in school? It is useless to demand better programmes. The glittering images kill time, and this is all that is asked.

In addition, the commercial exploitation of a generation believing itself to be, as advertisements claim, a special class, is permanent. It follows that, intoxicated by superficial notions before reaching the age of reason, young people lose the sense of their roots and imagine that they are living in their own world which excludes all older persons.

Their ears are closed to everything said by parents or family members.

They are unaware of a comment made by Madame de Sévigné: 'If people are born with two eyes, two ears and only one tongue, it is because they must watch and listen twice as much as they speak.'

They do not listen and do not see, but they talk, gossiping among themselves, debating things endlessly, holding interminable discussions, useless conversations.

In their impotence, educators – deans, administrators, and teachers – have forgotten their true vocation of teaching and educating the young. As a result, the inevitable has happened. The healthy and normal revolution which should have been encouraged from above is replaced by a disorderly revolt, sometimes voluntarily controlled.

There is no longer a union of heart and spirit between two generations, despite the fact that one was born from the other.

The West will transmit the Tradition of which it is the guardian by giving a new appeal to essential values, which must be respected if the Laws of Life are not to be violated. Tradition symbolizes the quintessence of human experience and is meant to be the foundation of what is now, in order to become what shall be.

The quintessence, the purest, most subtle essence derived from experience, is transmitted by Tradition. When its message is not adulterated and when, beyond the forms it may take, it is well understood, it leads to the discovery of an eternal wisdom which may be considered as a signpost on the path towards inner realization.

For those who follow this path, there will no longer be any broken or strained bonds. There will be instead a bond of heart and spirit, and an acute sense of freely accepted responsibility.

The contribution of all human beings to the proper functioning of society, and therefore to its economy in the exact meaning of the word, will call upon each one of us to measure his own contribution and to observe rigorously the fulfilment of his duties. These duties result from a collaboration among equals who have different roles according to their individual gifts.

Responsibility does not exist without the acceptance of a critical sense, which justifies the apparently privileged position of those who place themselves at the top of the hierarchy. There is no true privilege without sacrifice. This alone confers upon man his dignity. Therefore the

West, privileged by the gifts of nature, has the responsibility of accepting its vocation and of rejecting everything which degrades it.

CHAPTER 11

The Breakdown of Established Patterns

Everywhere triumphant, science continues its progress, leaving behind it a trail of problems which require ever new solutions.

Our knowledge increases continuously, but instead of furthering the understanding of the unity of the living whole, the Universe, it fragments whatever we have taken for granted, thereby conveying the idea of an ever greater complexity.

As a result, we are inclined towards specialization and organization. We wish to penetrate the hidden secrets of the universe. Relentlessly, we dissect the facets of our multiple discoveries, forgetting that organization needs to be part of an overall order.

Ideas contradict one another, concepts collide and words lose their meaning, being used to designate contrary aspects of things.

Science offers contemporary man a synthetic view of nature which, he believes, dispenses him from reference to traditional notions. His behaviour changes accordingly.

At this level, science becomes a transformative force, since the entire world is acquainted with scientific achievements through the omnipresence of information.

Information disseminates scientific discoveries, often in superficial, popularized form. Consequently, contrary to the postulates of science, which seek to study phenomena without attempting to derive meaning from them, pseudo-science causes those who are poorly informed to think that they are on the brink of a terrifying abyss or on the other hand, that they are omnipotent.

At each particular moment, science comprises the totality of human knowledge, but despite this fact it fails to provide the key to understanding.

Understanding derives from a supreme order and implies a sense of everlasting values, the multiple aspects of which must be grasped in their manifestations on all levels of existence.

Driven by our desire for power, we do not take the time to understand. However, our action should reflect the Supreme Order on every level. Turmoil and confusion are futile, even harmful, and since information plays an increasingly dominant role in the world, it assumes an ever-growing importance.

Since science opens the gateway to power, and can only evolve if information is constantly available to those responsible for progress, then obviously the science of information deserves particular attention.

As the mainspring of an evolving world, information penetrates everywhere. However, indispensable as it may seem, it does not constitute an end in itself. Unaware of this obvious truth, twentieth-century man has made information his god. Immense machines handle it, process it, manipulate it. These machines think in the place of human beings, reasoning logically and belching forth new data to serve as arguments for the most spectacular decisions.

Electronic brains decide in advance the outcome of

battles and inspire actions upon which war and peace depend.

This aspect, which is the other side of the technological coin, must be taken into account, since numerous abuses and even great dangers result from it. We are tempted to abdicate our free will and to bow before the decisions of robots, who take over.

In terms of their reaction to a signal, man and machine do have certain similarities of behaviour. Both react in a predictable manner to external stimuli. Exploitation of this behaviour is common and underlines the responsibility of those who manipulate the all-pervasive audio-visual media.

The use of advertising to provoke an automatic buying response is one of the characteristics of our times. Likewise, a crowd can be conditioned by the simple repetition of slogans which, as they are heard and repeated, eliminate the critical intervention of the mind and lead to behaviour in perfect accordance with statistical predictions.

A message which sets weak forces in motion may produce significant results. To achieve this, the message must trigger a series of effects which become more pronounced sequentially as in a chain reaction. Such is the case when space probes are electronically guided millions of miles from earth as well as when collective hysteria is generated by slogans repeated in cadence.

Therefore, the ability to escape the influence of electronically controlled action is above all the ability to free ourselves from a psychologically conditioned conscious or unconscious reaction, and thereby to escape from predictable behaviour.

A question still remains. Despite the growing complexity of the expanding realm of existence, can we act in full liberty so that our actions conform solely to intelligent criteria which we have chosen? Or has our world exceeded human measure, so that this is beyond our means?

The answer to this question can be found in an understanding of the relationships between our limited human capacities and the gigantic scale of the phenomena which stimulate our curiosity.

The brain gives priority to facts transmitted by the senses. Its momentary solution to any problem represents the means at our immediate disposal which enable us to organize our existence.

Might we then conclude that we are making poor, awkward or imperfect use of our senses? Certainly not. Instead, we are misinterpreting the information we receive, which we consider to be a precise and absolute expression of the reality of things rather than a representation of only one or a few aspects. Moreover, such aspects are subject to a constant transformation, and this situation does not make our search for truth any easier.

Only the awakening of the suprasensory – and therefore intuitive and inspired – faculties of perception, bringing about the adherence of the rational mind, can indicate the path to follow. Such is the meaning to be given to Royal Alchemy. It is the science of transformations induced by Cognizance, culminating in the development of a human type meant to be part of a civilization integrating man's scientific conquests and his spiritual aspirations. If these aspirations are repressed, they may lead to errors of the worst kind. Civilization should enable us to master the powerful energy at our disposal, energy which would produce disastrous effects in an unprepared world, consumed by greed, ravaged by fear and driven by the desire for power. To create this civilization, we must continue to develop the spirit of progress fostered by modern technology, while remaining faithful to the Eternal Wisdom which humanity has distilled during its long history.

The wise and intelligent human being would then be able to rise above the kaleidoscopic appearance of things and the deceitful glitter of false notions, mastering his thought instead of being mastered by it, practising intellectual broadmindedness as well as total tolerance.

A profound reversal of values would thereby occur, ushering in the new age.

Meanwhile, events are accelerating, the gears are overheating and a disaster seems likely. Blinded by an apparently limitless desire for power, we want the moon – but we want it for ourselves. Let the neighbour who tries to grab it beware!

Feverish efforts are being made to organize all aspects of existence, from the conquest of space to automobile traffic. But nothing is being put in order. Despite increasing numbers of traffic signals, a downpour can upset all expectations, producing traffic jams that enrage the driver. If existence is to be put in order and if excesses are to be avoided, we must begin at the beginning.

We think only about existing well without knowing why we exist. Because we imagine that we know many things, we believe ourselves to be intelligent. We claim to be constructing ideal societies while actually promoting confusion and incoherence.

Since order does not prevail, organization proves impotent. 'Well-Being' remains an illusion, while the low quality of our existence is accentuated. Information proliferates; devices travel through the skies; and extraordinary gadgets make all kinds of feats possible. From artificial satellites to the spies in thrillers, everyone is seeking information as a source of power.

What is the result? Nothing very impressive.

The trouble spots of the globe remain troublesome:

conflicts multiply and the gap between the 'haves' and the 'have-nots' is growing.

Can we escape from the vicious circle and make good use of the findings of our rapidly expanding science? Indeed we can, provided that we assign science its proper role, which is to serve humanity by fostering understanding. Information, properly interpreted, should promote this.

The meanings conveyed by words are the keys to understanding. We often forget that we are moving within a tower of Babel, which exists not only because linguistic barriers separate peoples, but also, and especially, because words can elicit a different understanding in the listener from that intended by the speaker.

The process which leads to understanding is unknown. We do know, however, that brainwashing produces spectacular results – a fact which is widely put into practice.

Research is being conducted to understand better the functioning of the human brain. Experiments in the United States on rhesus monkeys are instructive in many ways. It has been discovered that the brain of rhesus monkeys, which consists of two lobes like our own, transforms the perception of a white circle into the idea of food if the visual channel leads to one lobe, and into the notion of danger if it leads to the other.

It is possible, by sectioning some of the nerves leading from the eye to each of the two lobes, thereby separating the visual impressions into two separate channels, to reverse the phenomenon. A white circle: one of the monkeys grabs food, while the other flees for his life.

This is an image based upon biological reality. Yet how many times do we carry on impassioned discussions without realizing that the other person, relying on different notions, states in complete good faith the opposite of what we consider to be true?

The scientific upheaval of our day and age requires another form of understanding and a new language better adapted to the shifting realities of a universe in constant transformation. In this way it becomes possible to communicate exactly what is understood.

We witness daily transformations on many levels and, panic-stricken, we exclaim: 'Everything is changing; everything is different! Nothing we considered secure is exempt! The world is going mad!'

To reassure ourselves, we rely upon good principles as a guide to our behaviour, and in their name we kill one another. Good principles give a clear conscience. To admit that these principles might be good only in appearance would shake the very principle of principles itself, and so we prefer to avoid the issue even if the necessity for a complete mental upheaval becomes more apparent every day.

Was any principle better established or better accepted than that of universal gravitation? Celestial bodies rotated around the sun according to an energy determined by their respective mass and distance.

This world without mystery, this cosmos – a perfect example of a magnificent mechanism, the laws of which had been explored – formed a unity securely based on the determinism of predictable causes and effects. Gravitation apparently provided a key to the seven locks of the secret book of Nature – a metaphor for the Law of Laws making possible an explanation of the universal movement of Life.

Despite such certainty, a few minor difficulties emerged along the way. The void of outer space was bothersome, since the transmission of light rays could not be explained except by the presence of a medium which theoretically did not exist.

No problem! It was invented. Since the principle could not be questioned, ether was necessary, and so ether there was! Celestial bodies did not sense it – that would have slowed their movement – but light rays knew how to use it. Thanks to the ether, these rays reached us from distant galaxies.

Then came the experiment of Michelson and Morlay, two scientists who were curious about the mysteries of the elusive ether. They observed, to everyone's consternation, that ether was only a mental projection. A world of electromagnetic waves replaced it. A revolution!

The minuscule, the imperceptible, the invisible electron, inseparable from all matter, was sufficient to make the great cosmic clock break down!

The cosmos is not a mechanism; it is movement. Certainly, on the scale of our everyday world, Newton's laws remain perfectly valid, but everything changes when we approach the atomic universe of which this world is composed.

In the atomic universe, events occur without a determined or formal cause. An electron's behaviour is acausal. When rotating around a nucleus, it ought to lose its energy. It does not. An observer expects one thing and discovers another. In fact, he does not observe anything; he merely supposes that a certain cause will probably produce a certain effect. There is no assurance: causal determinism is replaced by the principle of statistical probability.

Oppenheimer, the great physicist who attempted to describe the difficulty caused by language – which is not suitable for atomic phenomena – said: 'To the most apparently simple questions, we either cannot give an answer, or we give one which at first glance seems like a strange catechism rather than the categorical statements of physics.'

Are we faced with a contradiction within science itself? No.

We are faced with the breakdown of the established thought patterns of classical science, a breakdown which requires a new formulation in order to provide an adequate basis for the logical reasoning of our era. In a strange way this substantiates the statement that incremental additions to knowledge never lead to Cognizance, which transcends it. Even so, knowledge must be expressed in a correct and understandable way.

'Science has discovered 'sin!' exclaimed a great physicist when he learned of the explosion of the atomic bomb at Hiroshima.

Science is not on trial! But science confers power, and it is we who have made bad use of this power. Although we wring our hands, we refuse to relinquish that which threatens to annihilate us. Not only is science innocent, but it can provide us with a perspective that reveals the eternal values of Supreme Order.

In many fields new vistas are creating different options, unsuspected possibilities for acting in complete independence. The opportunity to avail ourselves of powerful resources should encourage us to use them with great care.

It is interesting to note that the physicist Costa de Beauregard states that information, because of the order it produces in nature, counteracts the tendency of the cosmos towards entropy – that is, the cessation of all movement and therefore death.

Entropy, towards which the world is supposedly moving, seems the most probable state, since all movement slows down and ceases with time. However, the movement of Life continues without perceptible slackening, and that is no small miracle.

It would seem that, due to the energetic interactions in

the atomic universe which produce a constant adjustment among the particles of each atom, information can arrest the advancement of entropy and counterbalance the disintegration of energy. This fact upsets one of the fundamental principles of thermodynamics and also overturns the concept of determinism, which has been used often to justify inaction.

Since this fundamental statement opens up new horizons, it deserves a few moments of attention.

Once we realize its importance, we can accept freedom of choice; we can admit that each of us is master of his fate.

In fact Cognizance, based upon the correct interpretation and the proper integration of assembled information, makes possible a constant adjustment to circumstances, calling upon us to act in constant harmony with the Laws of Life and therefore with the laws of evolution instead of entropy.

This would mean that we ought to change our ideas of education. Super-specialization hampers the awareness which is indispensable for the intuitive perception of relationships beyond logical reasoning. Education should therefore be concerned with the development of Intelligence in the true sense of the word.

Such an approach seeks to discover the place of scientific research within a vision of cosmic order so that the latent capacities of the brain may be developed, allowing human genius to flourish for the benefit of the community, which is prepared to recognize the essential beyond the moving interplay of appearances.

Full employment, social security and increased buying power would then be possible in an economic order reflecting proper relationships between initiative and work, between financial means and the requirements of production, so that a balance could be achieved between the needs of all and the possibilities offered by the judicious exploitation of the resources of each country.

This harmonious balance could only be conceived in the context of a social, national and supranational justice based upon the equitable division of goods within nations as well as around the globe.

In this way, confusion, helplessness and fear would disappear. Science would play a role in evolution and true authority would assume its proper place.

Is this an inconceivable perspective or is it Wisdom reserved for the new age? The succeeding generations who ponder these questions will provide the answer!

Already their thought is following a different pattern from that of preceding generations.

As always in such cases, excesses occur. Although the intrinsic virtues of work, knowledge, clarity of expression and traditional attainments are at times rejected, these reactions will eventually subside.

Another aspect has to be considered. The relationships between men and women appear to be developing in a way which may deeply change certain basic assumptions.

The widespread acceptance of sexual freedom and eroticism has an effect upon the psyche which upsets certain notions previously considered to be indispensable for the closeness of a couple.

Group sexual activity, advocated from time to time, will not endure since it is against Nature, but monogamy as it is known today may undergo modifications.

A broader vision of the bonds of affection among members of a spiritual family will cause restrictive jealousy to be replaced by another way of seeing things. People will begin to understand that a pure friendship can develop between one member of a couple and a third party of the same or opposite sex, without harming the intimacy of the couple, especially if honesty replaces hypocrisy.

Such an evolution points toward a fraternal understanding extended to all members of a spiritual community and therefore toward an expression of essential values of which the nucleus would be the enlarged family unit.

CHAPTER 12

The False Élite

To take the path means to look deep into the eyes of people, to catch a glimpse beneath the veil which covers their wealth or their poverty, their griefs or their joys.

To follow the path means to attune the soul's rhythm to that of the Soul of the World. Such attunement to the most subtle vibrations, perceptible to the ear which does not heed the dissonant noise of a confused world, will generate understanding. Understanding calls upon those who take the path to accept the challenge which they must face.

In the preceding chapters, certain factors within our society have been considered as causes for an internal revolt and its consequences. Continuing our objective examination, we will now try to understand the implications of the challenge offered from the outside.

Political or sociological aspects of the problem will only be raised when necessary to clarify certain issues, our sole purpose being to maintain our unbiased perspective so that we are not blinded by any false notions.

However, let us not refuse to look at the confusion of the world since, instead of closing our eyes, we should see it clearly.

The West seems to be on the defensive. New

expressions have appeared in political language: we speak of puppet states or neutralist demonstrations when referring to aspects of the opposing blocs, East and West.

The Cold War and peaceful coexistence are the poles between which an unstable armed peace vacillates. Such a precarious peace is maintained by a balance of terror and not by Wisdom.

The balance of power in space, parity of conventional weapons, tactical balance and nuclear parity constitute a panoply of arguments intended to arouse or soothe passions. 'War', Einstein said, 'is a childhood disease of humanity.' Nothing could be more true, and if children refuse to grow up, they must realize that they incur the great risk of becoming victims of their immaturity.

How can they be made to understand this? Such is the dilemma – and we must not forget that conflicts tend to become generalized.

The North-South dialogue between the 'haves' and 'have-nots' is at cross-purposes. Guerilla warfare is rampant in Latin America, Africa and Asia. The economic crisis spreads, bringing suffering in its wake and, in order to mask internal difficulties, government leaders do not hesitate to engage in military adventures, imagining that the annexation of territory will stir the poverty-stricken masses.

The authority of the West is eroding and numerous are the methods being used to accelerate its decline. This situation gives grave reason for concern since everything causing deterioration is opposed to the fulfilment of a vocation meant to be spiritual in nature.

'Spirit against guns', one might say sceptically. Yet this may indeed be a possibility, provided that we are defending the intangible and the sacred, and provided that our resolve is sufficient to make any potential aggressor understand the futility of a conquest which fails to make the vanquished submit to the law of the victor.

Such was the case in the second world war. After Dunkirk, the British determination to avoid defeat was the nation's ultimate weapon at a time when most of the others had been left behind on the beaches of France.

Wave after wave of bombers did not break this resolve and, contrary to all logic, Hitler, undoubtedly sensitive to the psychological wall erected against his invincible armada, abandoned his invasion attempt.

This is merely one of a number of examples which could be drawn from the victories and defeats of peoples throughout the ages. These bear witness to the Great Tradition of Knighthood, which at certain turning points in history must be remembered anew.

This knighthood has little to do with medieval chivalry, nor does it imply a return to the behaviour of any particular period. What it actually means is the establishment in its proper place of an élite of Cognizance, and therefore of competence, whose throne has been usurped.

Competence is not limited to knowledge. Our current difficulties can only be remedied by appealing to devoted individuals whose qualities are appropriate to the circumstances. Choice requires great lucidity and great freedom of judgement, implying possibilities of action which do not easily conform to a false conception of democracy.

Although no miraculous remedy can be proposed, it will be the task of the society of the Aquarian age to develop a form of government which respects true competence, freed from the restrictions which elections in their current form impose upon those standing for office.

Aware of its responsibilities, democracy will

accommodate itself quite well to a division between power and the authority conferred upon the élite.

A false élite governs the world and obviously seeks to discredit through ridicule the very idea that a true élite might exist.

Reduction to the lowest common denominator is considered a panacea for all ills and, from within as well as from without, the insidious effort is intensifying to replace essential values by false notions, of which the counter-culture mentioned above is one example.

Since a term other than 'élite' is not easy to find, we must emphasize that the élite in question refers to an élite of Cognizance rather than one of money, blood or education.

Diplomas attest to knowledge and no one can deny the role or importance of such. However, knowledge is distinct from Cognizance, which integrates knowledge with understanding. Only these together open up a broad vision of the problems of Life based upon the notion of service and not upon the idea of profit, which is considered secondary, even if legitimate.

At all levels, profit is conjugated with the verb 'to have', and service with the verb 'to be'.

An élite exists only where all those who might claim to be part of it give proof of their capabilities and their devotion through their respective fields of endeavour.

A shepherd, perfectly integrated into the surrounding nature, aware of his responsibility to guard the flock and exercising this responsibility properly by leading the animals to shelter when storms threaten or by moving them to new pastures when necessary, belongs to the élite at his level.

He illustrates an essential aspect of the élite: the particular quality of an industrious, competent and autonomous individual who exercises his abilities and performs his responsibilities by means of decisions of which he is the sole judge.

When individuals are deprived of such possibilities they are enclosed in an environment which, despite its being characterized as 'popular', cannot be made attractive.

Indeed, the spirit of enterprise and liberty is crushed and civilization regresses as a result.

The industrious person, in the broadest meaning of the term, affirms himself as an individual. On all levels, his work implies careful reflection. It contributes to the development of the community, which establishes its value through the respect that its members have for one another, and therefore for the individual and his freedom of decision.

Liberty and dignity are the foundations for initiative, for research and, consequently, for progress.

An individual aware of his duties as well as of the fundamental reasons which justify them manifests a particular way of being.

Awareness and lucidity characterize him, encouraging him to take his place at the forefront of the world's stage.

Words are misleading, and the language of a tradition can be misunderstood by those who have discarded it.

In the past the term 'élite' referred to a privileged social class. However, words must be given their true meaning. The knighthood of earlier times also represented an élite. In neither case are these words meant to evoke what actually existed. Rather, both terms designate a universal tradition which appears in different historical periods. In all ages there have been knights: the kshatrias in India, the samurai in Japan, the knights of the Rose and the Cross in Europe and today all those on the path who seek to liberate the living forces imprisoned within themselves in order to open up to a different consciousness.

The search for a master, which we have noted as a characteristic of our times, reflects this quest, which is akin to the ideal of knighthood: an ideal of service beyond personal self-interest.

The false élite fails to recognize the true one. It usurps positions of power and rejects the idea of service. To help us understand the ideal of knighthood, which transcends time, we shall turn to symbols, allowing them to speak so as to avoid interpretations which falsify a vision intended to be free from all preconceived opinions.

In the chapel of the Knights of Malta in Rome, a painting represents the Grand Master of the Order. Let us forget the portrait itself in order to grasp the ideas which may emerge from it. These alone interest us as fundamental notions.

In the painting can be seen the globe, a symbol of the universe, the armour, a symbol of Wisdom, and the azure blue mantle, a symbol of mastery through Spirit.

The white lining to the mantle suggests purity and consequently invulnerability, and the eight-pointed cross affixed to the armour symbolizes the realized human being, regent of the Centre and of the Eight Horizons – in other words, of the centre and the four cardinal points as well as the four intermediate directions.

Interpreted in this way, the painting gives a clear idea of what has to be undertaken by Western man if he wishes to be the worthy heir of a legacy which is his due. By claiming it, he could awaken to glory, donning the sparkling armour and the eight-pointed star. However, no outward sign would be visible, since his armour could only be perceived by the individuals who in growing number seek to promote a civilization in the service of humanity, a civilization which would restore to its true perspective the notion of 'nobility of heart'.

The universe is entrusted to the care of humanity, and nobility of heart is a consequence of this reality. The flora and fauna and the wealth beneath the soil are not objects. To enjoy them entails an obligation to respect the balance necessary for the development of plant and animal species, and of minerals as well, since their transformations also obey the law of evolution.

Confusion and turmoil will not help us to respect this balance, since these are merely the expression of fear which every potential adversary can exploit.

The challenge which the West must face has many aspects. Established structures are being weakened, threatening to crumble. If this is to be avoided, lucid awareness is necessary. We must realize that when wars break out, men and women on both sides have agreed to wage them. Undoubtedly, they impose their will upon others, but even so, war is the expression of an inner conflict which also exists within those who consider themselves coerced to fight. Such inner conflict directs and feeds every confrontation.

Fanaticism and vainglory on the part of the belligerents enable them to forget their individual problems and difficulties, which they attempt to avoid by throwing themselves headlong into the fray. However, forgetting them only postpones the finding of solutions which do not appear once the war is over.

If we wish to pass sound judgement on the causes of confrontation, we must begin by resolving our own contradictions and conflicts. As long as this is not understood, and achieved, we are *all* responsible for *all* wars, for the actions which they provoke as well as for their consequences, since they are only external projections of whatever disturbs, constrains or frightens us.

An awareness of this fact would most certainly accomplish more than any demonstration for peace, which only reinforces a sense of satisfaction gained from the illusion of effective action – which might indeed be effective if freedom of assembly were accepted on both sides.

Since this is not the case, we must see things as they are and act accordingly.

CHAPTER 13

Primordial Liberty

Western structures are crumbling. It is time for all of us to awaken to the fact that fundamental values, of which we are the beneficiaries as well as the guardians, must be preserved before it is too late.

The mission of the West has always been, and continues to be, the promotion of the Art of Living, which is quite different from a mere technique of existence.

We exist intelligently or stupidly, passionately or sedately, sensually or wisely – in other words, in a personal, individualized way – whereas the Life we manifest in our own particular manner is universal.

It pulsates in everything that we see, touch, smell, perceive or express. 'Life is the light of men', state the sacred texts. In one of his works, Montaigne speaks of a science, 'the science of understanding how to live this life well and naturally'.

Words change, but the idea that they transmit remains the same. The Art of Living integrates knowledge with our innermost aspirations, liberating us from organized constraints, from technocratic excesses and from intellectual dogmatism, which hamper the creative forces which are a natural and spontaneous gift of Life. Encompassing existence and Life, the art of living serves as a bridge between the ephemeral and the eternal. It is founded upon harmony, and therefore upon beauty, which defies space and time and gives rise to the emotion of the soul as it becomes aware of the great mystery beyond the visible world.

In such plenitude, we can collaborate in the Great Work of Nature. In order to fulfil our destiny, we can practise the 'Royal Art' described by the alchemists – that is, the Art of Living.

We evolve as does our environment. Human evolution exerts an increasingly active influence upon the surrounding world. Conscious of being conscious, we human beings are the only ones on earth trying to submit the mineral, plant and animal kingdoms to our will.

We wish to be free, but are often unaware that the 'Royal Art' is based upon the Cognizance of a Law reflecting Supreme Order and Harmony without which no freedom exists.

We breed animals which provide us with abundant products for consumption. We cultivate plants, grains and vegetables; but can we claim that we have developed well-cultivated plants and well-bred animals?

Unfortunately not.

Chemical fertilizers and animal husbandry methods are intended to make a profit. They are not in keeping with the essential understanding of the Law of Harmony which entails a responsibility proportional to the power we have appropriated because of our wish to dominate nature.

We violate nature instead of obeying it, and our subsequent difficulties are a heavy price which we pay reluctantly.

Unresolved problems accumulate and multiply, as do psychological reactions, producing remedies which are inappropriate for today's problems.

We may have good reason to be concerned about our fate, immersed as we are in the world's confusion. We are not prepared to defend ourselves against the pressures of the ambient world and against the disorder caused by the accelerated rhythm of political, economic, scientific, technical and religious events. Our desire for possession seems to have led us astray from our real purpose. Greed in all its forms exists deep within us and we devotedly pursue everything which intensifies it.

Our activity is feverish and the value of human life becomes very trivial, being cheerfully sacrificed to any passion whatever.

Let us recognize this situation, understanding that despite periodic revolutions which seem to overthrow everything, mental inertia reinstates under new labels identical procedures which ultimately resolve nothing, despite the fact that they may benefit groups different from those previously in power.

Disoriented, victimized by our feverish pace, we cannot help exclaiming: 'Good Heavens, how quickly time passes! Only yesterday I was twenty years old and today I am four times that age. Have I lived?'

The final stage of our journey approaches, and anxiously we listen to the answer which surges up from within: 'You existed, but you were not truly alive.'

To be alive we must be conscious, harmonizing our behaviour with our inner reality which corresponds to transcendental reality.

We must dare to achieve a psychological revolution. The older generation, whose bodies and souls have been shaped by age and experience, should be able to inspire in youth, who are seeking their own path and purpose, hope in a human predestination which invites them to discover the Art of Living amidst the difficulties and constraints of daily existence.

Adolescents will then be reluctant to waste impetuously the opportunity which their youth affords them and they will look squarely at the future without fearing adulthood or old age.

In addition, we ought to rediscover the value to a community of the experience of old age. All too often nowadays we deprive ourselves of its benefits.

It is absurd to use flimsy social considerations as an excuse for eliminating men and women from active life at a time when they have reached the fulfilment of their experience.

Retirement, a long-desired goal for many, undoubtedly allows some to rest after an existence of hard labour and others to devote themselves to tasks appropriate for their aptitudes.

Unfortunately, this does not apply to the majority, who are despondent, resorting to whatever subterfuge they can, whether suited to their individual aptitudes or not, to escape feelings of uselessness.

This regrettable attitude of the community is contrary to the sense of evolution.

Retirement should allow the elderly to manifest the quintessence of their experience gained from past efforts, thereby creating an élite of experience. We should assign to those in old age the task of transmitting to others, according to their evolutionary level, their acquired abilities and their acquired understanding. Society would greatly benefit from this, and the longer lifespans made possible by medical care would find their proper meaning.

Those who gained maturity through the vicissitudes of existence would assume their true stature on their own level and, in due course, they would leave their body as one leaves a meal, with dignity.

Unfortunately, we have not attained such wisdom. So

we must learn to think correctly in order to avoid falling prey to ideologies bolstered by false notions. It is therefore essential to understand thoroughly the mechanism of thought. Mysterious in its complexity, thought is conditioned by different physiological, sensory and emotional factors, modified and influenced by memory, environment and beliefs.

Thought is based on assumptions, the value of which must be re-examined constantly. The knowledge which determines these assumptions varies continuously, and notions which were considered definitive correspond at best to the truth of the moment. It would be wise to heed the words of Plato: 'Our prison is the world of our perceptions.'

As prisoners of our perceptions of the world, we must have the courage to broaden them. If we are to think correctly, we must become aware of the spiritual secrets of the universe.

If matter can evaporate into light and if light can condense into matter, then a transcendental reality must be accessible behind the visible or invisible phenomena of our world. The eminent atomic physicist Max Planck in his statements reflects a similar view. He writes: 'As a result of my research on the atom, I can state the following: there is no such thing as matter itself. All matter comes into being and subsists solely as the result of a force which makes the tiny particles of the atom oscillate, assembling them into minuscule solar systems. Behind this force, we must admit the existence of a conscious and intelligent spirit.'

The reality of the universe is revealed little by little to those who seek it, but we must never forget that if we are to apprehend this reality, we must become free in order to recognize the Law and the principles which govern everything in existence. Once we have attained this certainty, the Art of Living will lead us to the discovery of the self and will enable us to adapt our behaviour and our actions to the continuously changing conditions of the world. Aware that at each moment we enter a new world different from the one which we have just left, we shall sever the links which tie us to the recent past and prevent us from opening ourselves up to the new impressions of each instant. Our thoughts will no longer be imprisoned by memory or by conservative attachments resulting from the psychological inertia which determines false behaviour.

In this nuclear age, we must understand that the Art of Living requires us to surpass our limits, whether psychological or of some other nature, in order to dissipate the shadows which hide us from ourselves.

Would this not be an inspiring task for the youth of the new age?

CHAPTER 14

Authority and Power

The bold suggestion that élites of Cognizance be established calls for an explanation.

It was implied earlier that we are actors on the world's stage, and that those who ought to take a leading role are absent. We might now add that we may be seeking them in the wrong way or in places where they cannot be found. Perhaps it is less a search than an expectation.

Expectation promotes numbness and inertia, especially if we do not know how to carry out our search and where to begin.

One thing seems clear. The degradation of our essential values cannot continue without risking the destruction of humanity. Directions for committing suicide, worship of sex, addiction to drugs and shameless exploitation of licentiousness under the guise of liberty – claimed to be the prerogative of modern youth – lead to inexorable decline.

Unless there is a constructive reversal, which cannot be achieved by mere prohibitions since these only repress what needs to be dissolved, the mission of the West will be irrevocably jeopardized. Only a better understanding of the laws of nature which reflect the transcendental order of the Truths of Life – an order to which we are subject – can bring about such a reversal.

To achieve it, we must discern the deep motivations ————ial interests of those involved before we can ————lutions. Acute perception is required to ————th external events the roots which cause ————rate.

————truth is needed to offset bitterness, empti- ————intment and isolation, which are some of ————omponents of an escape from ourselves – an ————n seeks morbid pleasure in destruction or ————ion.

————acy, a form of government which should be better understood, is to be perfected, it must transcend those defects which provoke reactions leading periodic- ally to dictatorship.

It should be possible to gain votes without resorting to the excesses of demagoguery and without inventing false justifications or dealing underhanded attacks to political opponents.

It should be possible to consult an assembly of com- petent individuals who have renounced all ambition, including the desire for access to key positions or to honours, an assembly of individuals able to devote them- selves to the well-being of those whom their advice would benefit.

Such has occurred in the past. It was because of this practice that Egyptian theocracy endured for thousands of years. The assembly of Amphyctions in Greece is another example; and it would not be totally absurd to conclude that the Japanese economic miracle is in part the result of peremptory counsels made by an association of retired chiefs of industry never seen but dedicated to the national interest, whose influence can be felt in every major resolution.

The appraisal which is man's due should therefore be related to his ability to enhance the well-being of his fellow man. This ability may lie at different levels. If, for example, it exists in the area of technological or scientific achievements, then the individual's scope of thought and action should be limited to this level.

The technological élites would maintain authority over those who work under their direction, whereas the authority of the élite of Cognizance would exert itself on another level. Thinking for themselves, mastering their intellect without submitting to any ideology – since this would result inevitably in the elaboration of theories or systems – the Cognizant élite would be liberated from restrictive bonds. This does not mean that in a period of technological and scientific achievement, the importance of the élites of competence should be underestimated. Quite the contrary. They must assume their professional task and affirm their authority in accordance with their abilities.

The élites of competence might band together in a series of groups corresponding to their qualifications. These would not be labour unions, which have a different role, but rather 'idea-sharing groups' at various levels of competence. Communications among the different groups would make it possible to develop a course of action promoting the general welfare of society.

From group to group a consultative hierarchy could be established to advise those in power at every level of economic, administrative, cultural or artistic activity. In this way, leaders could receive invaluable assistance in making decisions.

This is only a suggestion. However, it raises important questions. How can an élite be recognized? What are its characteristics? How can this title of 'élite' be justified?

Authority and Power

We cannot identify an élite by an enumeration of its titles and characteristics. Once its competence is acknowledged, an élite compels recognition by a faculty of comprehension which exceeds the ability needed to carry out daily activities.

It is our understanding of what makes us human that helps us recognize an élite, rather than our practical understanding of the physical world, which is only there to respond to our needs.

Intelligence, which makes an adaptation to all circumstances possible, prompts the individual belonging to the élite to serve humanity, to improve its conditions of existence, and to help it discover and affirm its abilities by facilitating suitable choices.

The individual of the élite is aware that each particular problem is part of a more general one. He will therefore seek the aid of those interested in the general problem who are able to help resolve it.

He will not choose them in the hope of gaining their allegiance, but will solicit their aid according to their aptitudes and their spiritual availability.

His serenity will protect him from reactions to which others, caught within the limitations of their concepts and false notions, may fall victim.

Devoting himself to the development of faculties which are appropriate to man, he will adapt to the shifting conditions of Life, being fully present at each instant, aware of the factors which determine freedom of choice. He will therefore be able to discover the suitable means for resolving the problems at hand.

Everything moves very quickly in this world where change is constant. The person belonging to the élite must abandon habits which hamper his judgement. He must be continuously vigilant, capable of adapting the proposed solutions to the changing rhythm of the

99

moment, in order to integrate them into the reality of each instant.

Only the person who has dissolved the veil of national, social, political, familial, religious or other conditioning can see correctly, think correctly and act correctly.

Obviously, his action may take many forms and can range from advice to an outstretched hand, from a smile to severity. He is recognized through his state of being, which indicates that he is capable of discovering and implementing the required solutions. This state of being, deriving from Cognizance – which includes competence and an understanding of human problems as well as the ability to decide – results not only in proper action but also in a judicious choice of all those persons who must collaborate to carry out such action.

Competence produces confidence among collaborators; confidence produces willing acceptance of the decisions required at a certain moment; and acceptance promotes spontaneous support and, consequently, the joy of accomplishment.

This joy contributes to the development of those abilities necessary to the completion of the work. In this way the individual belonging to the élite serves as an example and provides a model for those who wish to understand their own purpose and the meaning of their evolution.

Each and every person is summoned to this task, and each individual can select himself, provided he perseveres in the face of obstacles, and provided that he knows himself well enough to perform his action at an appropriate level in harmony with his aspirations, which indicate the path he must discover.

Once he has found the path, he must commit himself resolutely to following it. However, since there are conditions to abide by, a certain asceticism is necessary. Such asceticism is not of a constricting nature, nor is it a penitence. Properly understood, asceticism should foster the development of the faculties of perception, sensory as well as extrasensory – in other words, the awakening of the latent capacities of the brain.

CHAPTER 15

Asceticism, A Misunderstood Practice

A society built upon the values of the lowest common denominator will have difficulty in admitting that an élite of Cognizance might one day claim its place.

However, there are signs that something of this sort is taking place. Many psychological and physical methods resulting in altered states of consciousness are being explored by an increasing number of people. Yoga, Zen, meditation and relaxation exercises are examples of self-realization practices related to asceticism. The term's original meaning was 'exercise', and by extension this has become synonymous with 'purification'.

The spread of such practices expresses the conscious or unconscious yearning of individuals who wish to discover the path to an authentic spirituality.

Despite the fact that certain individuals err by adopting techniques which are not suited to their needs and that others hope to benefit on a merely physical level, the situation is symptomatic. An aspiration towards another kind of world is emerging. Therefore, it is important to understand that the particular interpretation fostered by Christianity has caused Western texts dealing with asceticism generally to falsify its initial meaning of 'exercise'. Whatever the form of Christianity, in Christian dogma asceticism has implied suffering glorified by the acquisition of merits. To be in a state of ecstatic contemplation could not fail to be rewarded by an eternity of happiness. This interpretation of the redemptive value of pain led candidates aspiring to a spiritual life to invent graduated levels of suffering, on physical as well as psychological levels.

Such disciplines certainly produced endurance, as well as a desire for even more difficult tests to prove the strength of vocation and the sincerity of their aspirations. Constant fasting, disagreeable food, rough clothing, excessive cold or torrid heat were only a few of the difficulties willingly faced.

Seen in this light, asceticism resembles stoic impassiveness leading to a certain self-mastery and to the strengthening of character. However, such practices do not improve the faculties of perception nor do they increase the availability of heart and soul. In spite of the fact that the ascetic may wish to acquire these qualities, their benefits will elude him.

Since it is in our bodies that we must carry out our work, practices based on physical stress cannot lead to the plenitude of authentic self-realization. Particular gifts and abilities can be overdeveloped by extreme means, but the revelations of genius, the awakening of unknown faculties, or ultimate illumination, are never the result of exercises poorly suited to spiritual purposes. This does not mean that we must never practise physical discipline, but rather that such exercises should foster the development of all gifts, for which a vigorous and healthy physical body is the best foundation.

The apprentice ascetic – in other words, the individual who is aware of his destiny and ready to assume it – must avoid being blinded by misleading promises of rapid advancement, whatever the chosen method. Too many pitfalls lie in wait to destroy and disturb his psyche. All too often, good intentions are followed by inadequate exercises, because the initial choice was not without illusion.

Asceticism must not degenerate into methodical repeated exercises which produce habit. On the spiritual level, as in everyday life, habit is an obstacle.

We should not try to create a new personality by relying upon constantly repeated exercises, since this hampers the transcendence of our limitations.

Whatever form it may take, asceticism should make possible a process of identification promoting an understanding of the essential unity of the world, a unity which can only be perceived when all mental projections, beliefs or opinions are discarded. Such identification requires the relinquishment of an egocentric attitude separating an individual from his surroundings. This relinquishment is the result promised by different methods of self-realization.

Obviously, methods leading to an ever more complete relinquishment are the most suitable ones, but only common sense should guide the choice of those methods appropriate to the attainment of spirituality, since our physical and psychological states must be taken into account as determining factors. The choice becomes all the more difficult because it must be made before we even discover the meaning of spirituality.

Prejudices, fixed ideas, impatience to reach a goal, the illusion of being privileged, and chance – a convenient word to convince ourselves of being guided when we fail to recognize circumstances which have provoked unexpected events – falsify the original data. The first step along the path of asceticism consists in recognizing their falseness and abandoning all apparent justifications for an inappropriate choice. The second step is the full and complete acceptance of our mistakes, if unfortunately such have been made. Continuing along the same erroneous path is contrary to the manifestation of Intelligence liberated from instinctive, emotional or intellectual conditioning.

If we abdicate our responsibility by basing decisions on reverence, a desire for approval, or belief in another's merits, we are seeking to be convinced that our decisions are right, and we are eliminating any critical sense which could help us avoid tragic errors.

Since every misapprehension produces anxiety, nothing is more logical than the wish to escape. However, it is a sign of immaturity to invent all sorts of justifications and to refuse the advice of those who could offer a warning.

No advice should be blindly accepted. However, it should be taken into account if it corresponds to a feeling which may have been unconsciously repressed.

A person who needs to justify his actions finds arguments in order to reassure himself. Such behaviour is contrary to self-knowledge and therefore hinders the awakening of consciousness, which makes it possible to see things as they are and to accept the consequences of our choice.

For the individual who practises it, true asceticism must never be a constraint, since a constraint accepted on this level becomes the breeding ground of pride. We might then think that we have acquired merit or powers which will give us pleasure. However, the acquisition of powers is only beneficial if these are used to foster proper human accomplishment, in which case they promote joy, a gift of Life rather than a desire for pleasure.

In all true asceticism, there is a search for an attunement with our innermost self, a search for love which erases all the blemishes of a personality eager for enjoyment or security, which hinder the development of this attunement.

Since asceticism means a detachment from everything which conditions the individual, it is a liberating choice. We must be free to approach truth, which is an internal value beyond definition. If such an internal value is to be perceived, self-awareness is required. Emotions, mental projections or illusions obstruct suprasensory perceptions, which transcend opinions or judgements and make possible a lucid appreciation of the essential. The object of all psychosomatic methods is to dissolve everything standing in the way of this appreciation. These methods require those who adopt them to be fully present, free of all preconceptions, clichés and opinions, and to adapt their actions to the conditions prevailing at each moment. A constantly renewed awareness of each instant characterizes such a state.

Liberated from the desire to attain any goal, the ascetic, who is far from being a penitent, is in no danger of abandoning his lucid vigilance or of yielding to the mirage of satisfaction. His constantly renewed awareness dissolves those limits and hindrances which prevent the expansion of consciousness. Detached from the past and from the future, he acts in the present. The eternal present is both within and without, and corresponds to the truth of the moment grasped by a full and complete vision of the relationships manifesting themselves on physical, psychological and spiritual levels, as well as of the interactions between the three levels.

Only a perfectly adapted asceticism makes us free, aware and worthy of assuming our vocation.

Such a vocation does not constitute a goal, but indicates a path of accomplishment. It does not depend upon a deliberate wilful choice but rather upon a mysterious sentiment which stimulates our will, helping us to achieve what is felt before being thought.

A vocation corresponds to a commitment which, if fully accepted, will transform the body into a faithful servant, able to express the comprehension which weaves a living bond of fraternity between everything existing, between man and the universe. Such a comprehension is indeed the true expression of Love.

CHAPTER 16

From Competence to Cognizance

Given the present rhythm of evolution and the intelligence that it requires, a profound worldwide reform of governments and institutions is essential.

Who better than we in the West, with all our unsurpassed wealth of experience and ability, could draw the necessary conclusions and at least propose, if not implement, such a reform?

If we in the West agree to this task, then the short- and long-term consequences of such a decision will change the face of things, allowing us to avoid the convulsions which might destroy the civilization we created and which might cause us to perish in its fatal disintegration.

At present we are prisoners of words which have lost their meaning. The idea of democracy is based upon arguments diametrically opposed to one another. This can be explained by the fact that the term is formed from the Greek words 'demos', meaning 'people', and 'kratos', meaning 'power'.

The masses have power but lack authority. It follows that those holding the power of elective office assume a false authority, interpreting the meaning of this ambiguous word according to their whims.

However, the era of ideological interpretation is over.

The world is entering the era of Intelligence of the Spirit, which Teilhard de Chardin has called the Noosphere, open to all those aware of their essential task. Let us not forget that 'essence' is derived from the Latin word 'esse', 'to be'.

The state of 'Being' obviously implies that the necessary reforms must be inspired by Intelligence freed from any false notions which may have become ideologies.

In the name of ideology we fight each other. In its name, bombs explode and kill people who have no part in any terrorist plot. The terrorism of the right is indistinguishable from the terrorism of the left, and there is no evidence that the left is any less conservative than the right. Both sides are attached to 'irrefutable arguments' which belong to the débris of the past. Both sides cling to their arguments, wanting above all not to be wrong, hoping to avoid impugning their good conscience which claims to be defending a just cause – their own, of course.

Although it is certainly difficult to relinquish well-entrenched habits, we must do so if we hope to create a harmonious environment which allows human qualities to flourish. These alone should serve as building material for a viable society.

Therefore, we must be able to define the kind of environment in which we can be naturally useful to our society, and without which we cannot achieve self-realization. As Socrates said: 'Society is created because of the powerlessness of each individual to be self-sufficient, and because of his need for many things.'

To be effective in society is to be competent, and competence is based upon a profession or trade which requires a spirit of inventiveness and develops personal initiative and solidarity.

Industrious activity brings out the qualities necessary for the perfection of our abilities. It facilitates the integration of the individual into an orderly community in which each one is assured a suitable role.

The path which leads from competence to Cognizance thus becomes visible. By the force of circumstances, the awakened human being will be called upon to exercise his authority in the heart of the community, which will accept this authority since it is needed for the community's development.

Certainly, there is a great gap between an idea and its implementation. None the less, it may be useful to outline the foundations for a more fraternal and open world, if only to help us become aware of the need to break free from the limitations of false notions and so finally to change ships instead of wandering from port to starboard on the same vessel despite the futility of the effort.

Civilization cannot exist when we fail to comprehend the world in its totality. A superficial view of the world causes us to misunderstand, and therefore to confuse, authority and power.

Since our insufficient understanding provides an inadequate foundation for our physical, psychological and spiritual evolution, the world becomes the scene of incessant struggles in which social, national or political problems are mere pretexts.

We must therefore begin by putting things in their proper order. If we assure each individual an existence worthy of the Being that he is, he will be able to discover himself.

We pride ourselves on a technology which is miniaturizing a growing number of electrical and mechanical components, claiming correctly that these achievements represent progress. Today, we also need to miniaturize our commercial and industrial enterprises, since progress requires it.

If such were to occur, personal initiative, human

relations and ingenuity would prosper. The misdirected power of trade unions would be channelled constructively, naturally instead of by force, and efficiency would occur as a result of the development of creativity rather than because of the constraints of rationality.

The constant preoccupation of business and industrial leaders would then become to maintain creativity at an optimum level, since it would be their responsibility to co-ordinate the efforts of each individual and to foster a team spirit, enhanced by mutual confidence gained from the development of neglected abilities.

Such a process is taking place. In the United States as well as in Japan, large organizations have begun to break apart into small groups. This development will prove to be irreversible.

A collaboration among individuals to accomplish a task inevitably requires a hierarchy of values. In such a collaboration, each must assume his task as part of the whole, and the purpose of the whole must be clear.

In this way the new era will be different from the present one. Authority will be based upon Intelligence, which supplants purely intellectual concepts. The individual imprisoned by his intellectual limitations and by the ideologies he uses to ensure his supposed supremacy must yield to the individual who has developed his faculties of intuitive and inspired perception. These faculties generate ideas adapted to the circumstances of the moment, and by that very process gain the adherence of intelligence and therefore of the rational mind, so that whatever has been intuitively perceived can be verified.

The constant innovations of intelligence produce a beneficial creative rhythm. The person of authority will know how to develop such a creative rhythm and will be able to assume the responsibility which befalls him as a member of an élite of Cognizance.

111

Those in positions of social, political and economic power will be forced to heed the advice of persons whose major concern is the well-Being of the community, especially when they content themselves with acting as advisers.

On the physical level, science would attempt to discover the True. On the level of morals and ethics, the Good would coincide with our innermost aspirations and, in the realm of art, the Beautiful would transmit the vision of a transcendental reality.

Such a reality is not essentially different from the one revealed by religions, provided that the term 'religion' is taken to mean a link relating human beings to one another beyond all dogmas or interpretations.

Since we have mentioned art, let us add that art bears a message. In fact, the work of art implies harmony and becomes thereby an element of comprehension and elevation.

In ancient times, to abandon oneself to a work of art in the temples of Egypt was considered a religious act, since art alone makes possible the expression of highly spiritual themes. It forms the sensitive tissue of the human soul, so that we might say that the Art of Living is without doubt the supreme art.

If economics, politics and sociology are to foster the development of an Art of Living reflecting the perfect order upon which it is based, the individual of the élite must assume his proper place, remaining aware of the supremacy of Intelligence freed from passionate or emotional constraints.

If enough awakened individuals were to join together, offering the best of themselves in a common endeavour, then the miracle of an authentic Renaissance would occur and the mission of the West would be fulfilled.

CHAPTER 17

Science and Metaphysics

The development of a fraternal civilization, which it is the West's mission to promote, must be founded upon a vision adapted to the problems of our times. Such a vision must also take into account the heritage of humanity's collective past experience.

The spirit of progress resulting from scientific research cannot develop unless it is based upon Eternal Wisdom, which provides a continuous renewal of form and expression for the experience of humanity during its long history.

Technological achievements, which radically change the way of life for the planet's inhabitants, must therefore comply with the requirements of well-Being which emerge from our awareness of Eternal Wisdom.

In the new age which is dawning, women are undoubtedly meant to play a predominant role, provided they do not seek to imitate men. On the contrary, by exalting their femininity, they can express intuitive and inspired qualities which, in men as well as in women, are an expression of the creative aspect of the Eternal Feminine.

Intuitive and inspired qualities will serve as a counter-balance to the extreme development of the intellect –

although the role of intellect still remains paramount provided it is not allowed to impose itself as a proud master.

Through a harmonious balance between the rational mind on the one hand, and intuitive and inspired faculties on the other, the union between the two natures in each person can be achieved. Such a union invites us to take part in the Great Work, fully aware of the rhythm of evolution, of the requirements of the times and of our individual abilities, which we must not exceed.

Liberated from psychological constraints and from the fear promoted by attachment to rules, notions and doctrines, the awakened and thinking individual will perceive the essential, remaining lucidly aware of the truth of the moment.

Such awareness is a metaphysical act bringing about the dissolution of the barriers erected by the conceptual world. As a result, a psychological, chemical and bio-logical transformation takes place which fosters an understanding of the reasons for human existence on earth. When this occurs, we do not question; we grasp the obvious through a previously unknown faculty.

Metaphysics is the science of primary causes. Only an understanding of primary causes can be transformed into awareness, greatly aided by inner silence, which makes it possible to perceive that which 'Is' at each instant.

All forms of meditation tend to promote this possi-bility. Meditation, which has been practised since time immemorial, is obviously more than a simple exercise of silence; it is an act which is deeply rooted in the human psyche.

As the Gospels say: 'The kingdom of heaven is in the deepest part of the soul and can only be reached through love.'

Love is understanding, and to understand the essence of a particular phenomenon requires true intelligence and, indeed, an act of faith.

There was a time when there was no distinction between metaphysical, technological, philosophical and scientific domains. Today, it is necessary again to eliminate such distinctions since all their different aspects converge into a single reality.

The reduction of matter into elements, particles and waves has not resolved the mystery of manifestation or the mystery of our origins, despite the growing interconnection between metaphysics and physics.

Max Planck refers to God as creator of an order reflected by the smallest atom. Other equally eminent physicists speak of a fundamental source which is the origin of a universe not made of physical substance. According to Einstein elementary particles, the building blocks of matter, are only regions within which space-time takes on a particular curvature. This statement eludes any mental representation.

In a different way, the same things have been said before. In the eighteenth century, Berkeley, philosopher and archbishop, declared that the firmament and everything on earth only existed in our consciousness and that as long as things which apparently existed were not perceived by a consciousness, they only existed in the heart of eternity. Two thousand years before him, Democritus had already affirmed the same thing.

In our day and age, nothing justifies the separation of science, philosophy, religion and metaphysics. The Universe is One, Truth is One, and the Tradition is of a single origin. Different interpretations have been necessary to render it accessible to people of different cultural evolutions. These interpretations have often collided, creating apparent contradictions among the messages of great beings such as Buddha, Zoroaster, Confucius, Lao Tzu, Pythagoras and so many others.

These five initiates preceded and prepared for the coming of Jesus who, through his sacrifice, infused the Tradition with an aura of love so as to reveal to the world its unifying power.

Knowledge, which has been especially developed in our era, should promote a search for the profound meaning of the transitory and yet continual passage of human beings on earth. An exploration of the pitfalls of existence undoubtedly leads to the comprehension of an essential truth, an expression of the Law of Life to which we must submit through Wisdom. Knowledge in itself is barren, but when blended with understanding it confers upon human, social and political relationships an order reflecting transcendental harmony on the earthly level. From this perspective, during the past two thousand years, the development of the West has responded to the requirements of evolution.

Without much exaggeration, it could be said that Roger Bacon was the one who offered humanity a method of investigation and research which opened the way to our scientific and technological era.

Nicknamed the 'admirable doctor', Bacon, an English monk, was undoubtedly the greatest scholar of the thirteenth century. At Oxford and Paris he studied mathematics, astronomy, philosophy, medicine, physics and chemistry, none of which prevented him from conducting experiments to find the Philosopher's Stone; quite the contrary.

Endowed with an innovative mind, he inquired into universals, freeing himself from the restrictive interpretations of the teachings of Aristotle, and celebrated with enthusiasm the 'Scientia-experimentalis', which he wished to make active and scholarly.

He was accused of magic, sorcery and of relations with the devil. Thanks to the intervention of his former disciple Pope Clement IV, he was able to pursue his scientific work. However, at the death of his patron he was again thrown into prison, from which he emerged only shortly before his death.

At the time of his first imprisonment, he was kept under constant surveillance in a Franciscan monastery. The former secretary to Saint Louis, Cardinal Guido Fulcodi, an enlightened man who had heard that Roger Bacon might have access to the secrets of nature and that he had made astounding discoveries, wanted to meet him. The Franciscan superior, convinced that the prisoner's scientific curiosity was a sign of diabolic influence, prevented him from doing so.

Therefore, the cardinal sought an intermediary, which he found in the person of a devoted monk, Raymond Laon. Thanks to this subterfuge, he became aware of the importance of Roger Bacon's work, but did not dare ask for the prisoner's freedom until he himself became Pope Clement IV.

This overview is necessarily succinct, since many details are beyond the scope of our investigation. Instead of enumerating the currents of thought and their ramifications in Western scientific evolution, we will merely emphasize certain important turning points.

It was Roger Bacon who suggested that man consider as part of his experimental domain everything which could be directly observed, everything accessible to his investigation. He prepared the way for the Cartesian paradigm, which used assumptions established by thought as starting points, but considered them rational only if thought and observation coincided and could be verified by experimentation.

Roger Bacon did not separate philosophy from science

any more than did Descartes or Newton. They all contributed to the development of a philosophical era based upon experimentation, enlarging the scope of their thought beyond the experiments themselves in order to discover what they concealed. The domain of philosophy thereby became a scientific one which was convincing to the rational mind.

Experimentation was in no way contrary to a spiritual or theistic attitude, and Ora et Labora, the 'pray and work' of the alchemists, remained the foundation of research, permitting man to develop his innermost Self through the discovery of the laws of manifestation.

The Philosopher's Stone, the goal of the Great Work, revealed itself quite naturally in the mind of Roger Bacon, beyond the results of experimentation.

Subsequently, the situation changed, perhaps because of the vain pretensions of certain researchers inclined to pit science against spirituality, atheism against metaphysics.

Neither Francis Bacon nor Descartes committed such an error, nor did Laplace or others like him.

In the seventeenth century Francis Bacon, minister of Queen Elizabeth I of England, went so far as to affirm that every thinking mind should be open to science and to philosophy. The acceptance of this idea gave birth in London to the Royal Academy of Sciences.

But let us proceed methodically, without getting lost in details.

CHAPTER 18

The Desire for Certainty

Before the modern era, which future generations will regard as scientific and technological, learned persons were simultaneously philosophers, craftsmen, alchemists, astrologers and magicians. The etymology of the word 'magic' is connected to the Sanskrit root 'maj', meaning 'major', and magic was therefore considered to be a major art.

Astrologers, thaumaturgists, alchemists and magi were adepts of a major science, the science of the mysteries of nature.

According to ancient writings, they employed methods and had access to secrets which have been lost and never rediscovered. Although many of these were the secrets of initiation, they were none the less based upon a very advanced knowledge of the laws of nature and of how to handle them.

Working on different levels, the magi of the past belonged to initiatory societies and were sworn to secrecy for spiritual and ethical reasons so as to avoid wrong interpretations The evolutionary spiral of humanity's development had not yet attained the level at which progress would require advanced technologies and the ability to use them.

It was only in the seventeenth century that the transition from the age of craftsmanship to the scientific era began. From this moment on, it became increasingly evident that every thinking person had to be knowledgeable in science in order to benefit from its discoveries, which made existence easier. Such a situation resulted in materialism, which is nothing more than a dogmatic reaction against the apparent obscurantism of ideas imposed by theologians claiming to be the sole depositories of revealed truth.

Attached to their prerogatives and determined to impose upon others their domination and authority, which they considered indisputable, these theologians forbade all discussion and treated any thinking individual as a heretic.

They failed because of their ignorance, imagining they were the only ones able to interpret truth. However, materialism also failed, and continues to fail, in its opposition to obscurantism, in the same way and for the same reasons. Today ideologists lack neither virulence nor fanaticism, nor do they refrain from trying to exterminate 'insane' adversaries who foolishly refuse to embrace wholeheartedly their ideas which promise happiness for tomorrow.

Although materialism merely represents an excessive reaction against a theological world view, it will not disappear, since numerous methods and circumstances foster it.

The materialist creed, which only accepts as true that which can be demonstrated, confirms the scientific one, but it also serves as an obstacle to our aspiration to find Truth without recourse to any dogma. Our refusal to accept theological statements which do not coincide with our innermost feelings can create a psychological vacuum. This works to the advantage of ideologists, who make use of our apprehensions and uncertainties to impose their ideas upon us. What could be more natural than to cling to an ideology in order to escape the discomfort of doubt?

The desire for certainty explains why, at a given moment in history, man could imagine in good faith that science would have an answer for everything. Scientists wished to offer humanity the magic formula encompassing all the phenomena of nature, including the human one.

Although this formula has not yet been found, the scientific era has given birth to a type of individual who tries to make his own decisions according to his experiences.

This trend explains the proliferation of small groups or communities attempting to pool their experiences in order to discover together a reason for living.

The scientific era directs individuals towards areas of research where experience, if it is not distorted by imagination, is intended to complete, prove and validate assumptions.

Assumptions can certainly be improved, clarified and re-examined, but the individual of the scientific era only accepts that which seems satisfying to his reason. That is his strength and his weakness. His strength lies in the fact that the type of reasoning advocated by the scientific method, supported by a demonstration which can be repeated to verify the observed effects, awakens a critical sense.

Trained in this way, he will only accept as true what has been demonstrated. Such a critical attitude can develop an individual's capacities for discernment, and if he possesses a certain degree of scientific honesty, it can foster qualities which are opposed to all sectarianism. In the past, this would have been called humility.

The other side of the coin is the difficulty encountered by the same individual in admitting that the inconceivable might happen. However, science is forcing his hand. Scientific doubt implies a recognition of the possibilities inherent in nature for manifesting previously unknown laws.

The scientifically trained individual has denied miracles – which have indeed occurred – for too long to admit now with ease that 'psi' phenomena are the product of unknown energies, or that esoteric healing, whether by faith or by the laying on of hands, belongs to a vast occult domain having an obvious reality which cannot be rejected.

Thus, his faculties are challenged by the colossal task of exploring a vast terrain. To awaken to Cognizance, to master the laws of nature, to apply these laws and to play upon the occult keyboard of invisible energies – are these not challenges worthy of his abilities? Are they not worth accepting?

Today the materialist creed is being questioned despite the fact that, although it denies transcendence, it tries to adapt its theories to metaphysical requirements in circumstances where the phenomena escape observation.

We should be aware that 'awakening' is synonymous with 'initiation into the mysteries of nature': in other words, it is the acceptance of the Law which derives from Supreme Order.

It is true that scientific doubt can lead individuals on a path toward awakening. The release of immense energies, the conquest of outer space and the exploration of the moon all have beneficial aspects in several ways.

They are beneficial because they exalt the spirit of enterprise and enable us to transcend our limits, thereby promoting our self-realization.

However, if we aspire to power, the energies liberated by science may act destructively, transforming themselves into malevolent forces which threaten to destroy us.

Although we should not become alarmist, do we know that twenty million hectares of forests are disappearing annually? Do we know that the tropical countries are being deforested, that water will become scarce, that the extinction of plant and animal species is accelerating and that the concentration of carbon dioxide, as well as the depletion of ozone, will change the atmosphere of the upper layers and influence the Earth's climate? Do we know that this is only one aspect of the generalized deterioration of the conditions of existence on this globe?

We do know the facts, but we think we can have a clear conscience by pretending not to!

On the other hand, we forget that scientific doubt ought to benefit humanity. It can and should help us to let go of everything which must be left behind. It can and should help us to cast aside established notions and re-examine whatever we have considered definitive. Then we could gain a greater understanding of apparently insoluble problems which have been avoided or incorrectly perceived.

Scientific research reveals the complexity of the energetic interactions which, like Ariadne's thread, unite the phenomena of the cosmos and the creative principle – that is, the dynamic principle governing evolution on earth – together in the rhythm of life.

The source of our error lies in the attempt to transform scientific research into a closed technocratic system measuring everything in terms of a technology which has no recognition of spirituality and no understanding of a superior logic governing both man and the universe.

Although the scientific method enables us to attain

123

specific goals and to make certain discoveries, it does not in itself constitute a universal key.

The universal explanation of the reason, the meaning and the purpose of manifestation can only be found beyond all methods. Science requires us to observe in order to attain knowledge, and metaphysics invites us to discover the relationships so that we may understand. Since knowledge and understanding lead to Cognizance, the scientific method represents one aspect of human development, which in today's world marks a turning point in humanity's evolution.

The belief that science represents an end in itself is an idea which limits our possibilities and resources.

Scientific investigation opens up new fields and interests which are different from those of antiquity, the Middle Ages or the Renaissance.

Let us therefore thank science and bow to human genius, a reflection of the original genius which developed it.

CHAPTER 19

Are We Mad?

When constant dissatisfaction spreads and persists in social, political, national and international matters, and when the force of events threatens to push the world to the brink of disaster, then the situation clearly needs to change. In particular, a certain state of mind must be attained if anything worth while is to be accomplished.

An overview of our world's problems can help us understand their complexity as well as their interrelatedness, and may enable us to discover the elements needed to promote change.

The predominance of the West during the past two thousand years should encourage it to take the initiative for such change. If it fails to do so, serious consequences will ensue today and tomorrow, here and elsewhere.

How should we act? How can we reconcile the wisdom gained from the experiences of a long past with the pressing demands of daily life, which should not be ignored? Such are the questions which must be squarely faced. They lead directly to the problem of education, and require first and foremost understanding on the part of parents, to whom falls the heavy burden of educating the minds of children without deforming them.

The environment plays a major role in the learning

125

process, since the nervous system of the newborn exists only in a rudimentary state and his recently formed brain cells respond at first only to external and internal sensory impressions.

What do parents and society contribute to the incredible alchemy of this being's development as he grows up? Noisy arguments, sexual excesses, conflicts, bad faith and violent economic, social, political and athletic competition.

Are we mad? Are we criminals to project our vices so shamelessly on to the television screen, or to fill our newspapers with stories illustrating our lowest instincts?

Perhaps we are merely ignorant of the implications of our carelessness. We only see the surface of a world in turmoil, without penetrating to the roots of the evil which is sapping the vital forces of the planet.

We teach many things to our children, without having them learn the essential: what they are, where they are going, how to die not only physically in a distant future, but at every instant to the false impressions resulting from our torments and our fears.

Confusion and ignorance permeate the unconscious mind of the adolescent, who transforms the perceived disorder, which he wishes to escape, into the desire to build an ideal society, without yet understanding that such an endeavour must begin within himself.

In their ignorance, parents perpetuate disorder by thoughtlessly behaving in ways which assail the psyche of the child.

The neurons of a child's brain are affected by the dissatisfaction resulting from an abundance of goods available to feed his desires. The malleable qualities of his brain are such that it absorbs false notions like a sponge.

All too often this is forgotten. However, a healthy

reaction is now occurring. The wish to be useful has taken hold of the minds of the younger generation.

Such a wish generally develops at the age where an adolescent must make a choice at the end of his studies. The choice is complicated by economic difficulties which appear periodically, and these difficulties create a state of confusion, as shown by comments like the following: 'Nothing seems attractive to me. If only I knew how to go about reconciling my ambitions and my aspirations!' 'I would like to be useful to others, but I know how childish this wish appears when there is no possibility of doing so.'

These are only two examples among many. It is not easy to explain to a generation in search of itself how to escape from the impasse, how to discover its own deep inner reality and, consequently, how to make use of its abilities and gifts through judicious development. To choose one activity rather than another as a means to foster our own development and not as a way to earn a living upsets accepted ideas of comfort, profitability or appropriate behaviour.

The selection of individuals to fulfil specific functions in all fields should be based upon the candidate's devotion to duty and upon the importance the position would have for his development.

If this were the case, the conditions of existence for all members of society would improve, thereby increasing the appeal of any particular function. This improvement and appeal would exist not only at the level of professional endeavour, but also, and especially, at the level of human relationships. Everyone would undertake his activity not simply out of economic necessity but out of a wish to be useful, and therefore to be of service.

The wish to be useful is a powerful driving force for evolution. The question of unemployment and of the apparent uselessness it creates, which places a heavy psychological burden on those out of work, must be considered with great care.

It is more important than ever to find adequate remedies to this problem, since the accelerating rate of industrial automation frees us from a great number of tedious tasks – a desirable occurrence provided that we are offered an alternative path of fulfilment.

Such an alternative can only be conceived within the framework of an activity appropriate to our own particular level of competence. This activity should enhance the public welfare – a notion which must be better defined. In view of these considerations, society ought to acknowledge the value of any achievement, even if such an achievement is self-imposed.

It is not easy to resolve the difficulties of this complex problem in a brief discussion. However, it is clear that unemployment benefits offer an inadequate solution.

If we deny the urgency of the situation, we are ignoring an obvious fact which will inevitably require attention. Even if no viable solution can be suggested at this time, an examination of the problem will ultimately help the indispensable answers to emerge.

Whether we make certain suggestions advocating humanism or promoting change, these can only have meaning if we see the world as it is and human beings as they are, instead of imagining that ideology of any kind might meet the needs of the situation.

Therefore we ought to learn from the experiences of the past in order to anticipate the means to be employed in the future.

All the forms of government adopted in Europe were tried either in Greece or Rome. The diversity of governments has made it possible to choose a form appropriate to the temperaments of peoples and their leaders.

The criticisms of any particular form of government are of little importance, since lessons can be drawn from the diversity of the attempted experiments. These can be summarized in one sentence: 'Good government is based on a true adaptability of those governing to those being governed.'

When Solon established the Republic in Athens, the first measures he took were intended to defend the interests of the merchants. What was necessary then may also be necessary today, provided that merchants, tradesmen and industrial leaders awaken to their human responsibilities. All professional activities should help develop a sense of responsibility, and management must go beyond the limits of its particular functions in order to become harmoniously integrated into a larger whole. Obviously a new approach must be found and new relations must be created among professional fields which seem to be in competition with one another.

This does not mean that we should rethink economics: distinguished minds have already examined the problem. Rather, we should see things as they are. Since the elimination of competition undermines individual motivation, we must admit that competition also has a positive side.

On the other hand, fighting each other relentlessly and using questionable methods to beat the competition constitute negative aspects. Is there a middle course?

To fulfil their proper function, merchants, managers and financiers should be individuals of the Cognizant élite, qualified and disinterested so as to eliminate any rivalry of functions, cultures or social spheres. In this way, their professional competence would equal their human value.

Although this proposal will certainly give rise to understandable doubts on the part of the reader, hope is not a prerequisite for effort, nor is success necessary for perseverance.

In our day and age, we expect a statesman to have all the necessary qualifications except those qualities which are specifically human, since these would make him vulnerable.

A fundamental error!

One primary human quality is that of discernment free from all preconceptions. Such discernment does not excuse us from firmness when the defence of fundamental values demands it: quite the contrary. Consequently, a statesman can be defined as much by what he is not as by what he should be.

A statesman is not a priest. He is not called to the leadership of a country to blame anyone for past wrongs, nor is he meant to predict happiness for those faithful to him. He must govern; in other words, he must act so well that all the wheels of state function harmoniously, interlinked in the best way possible. He must be able to prove that events substantiate his policies. Therefore, he must think correctly. Foresight entails adaptability. To adapt to circumstances must not be considered as a betrayal of any particular doctrine, but indeed as a useful measure.

The governing statesman is detached from the past and does not dream of the future. Rather, he takes past experiences into account in order to act in the present and foresee what lies ahead.

A governing statesman does not wish to put any personal opinions into practice. He refers to things as they are, taking into account different trends of thought, the virtues and vices of men and women, and the relations his country maintains with the rest of the world. Destroying nothing, he uses everything for the well-being of those he governs.

He surrounds himself with collaborators whose

freedom of spirit equals his own. He makes decisions inspired by his competence, or better still, by his Cognizance, certain that these decisions will be understood by his collaborators who must implement them.

Undoubtedly, this is an idyllic picture. However, it is also a non-utopian vision of the future, since the world cannot continue on its current downward path which, unless there is a spectacular reversal, will precipitate it into the abyss of a global cataclysm.

In ancient Greece, the governing statesman considered himself the direct descendant of the gods. This was a convenient way to establish his authority on a firm basis, but it was dangerous, since it justified or masked incompetence.

A statesman must govern with authority, yet allow free expression of liberty.

Paradoxically, it could be said that he should use his authority to impose measures which will assure the maximum liberty – which is not to be confused with licence.

To govern is to be aware of a constantly shifting reality. Every measure which is suitable at one moment may prove false at a later date. The most praise-worthy intentions will appear inappropriate if the circumstances which made them desirable have changed.

The governing statesman must be mentally available so as to implement whatever policy needs to be implemented. He will respect traditional customs and will refuse to base his power upon the police or the army. His merit will result solely from his human qualities and from his intelligence.

Intelligence will direct him to follow the disinterested advice of an individual or of a group of individuals. Once he accepts their competence and authority, translating the advice they have given at his request into judicious acts, he will assume his full stature!

CHAPTER 20

The Initiatory Path of the West

Let us state as an axiom that an individual of the Cognizant élite is someone who is aware of the realities of the moment, whether these are visible or invisible; he is someone who acts according to a hierarchy of values, which he attempts to render perceptible at a level beneficial to everyone.

He will therefore try to foster a consciousness which, on professional, social, economic, financial or political levels, corresponds to a principle inherent in human thought. If not perverted, thought reflects a transcendental order necessary for the human constitution, in which the three levels – physical, psychological and spiritual – must be harmoniously integrated and thereby balanced.

Philosophically, it could be said that everything encompassed by transcendental order is reflected by human thought, if its rhythm reflects the rhythm of the soul, the vital element of the three levels.

Order mirrored in this way necessitates a hierarchy of priorities which prevent excessive specialization from promoting the over-development of one particular aspect or department of society at the expense of another.

The awakened individual, aware of the reality of the

moment, will seek to integrate each particular problem into the vision he has of the general interest, without allowing any personal or sectarian preference to falsify his judgement.

If we are not to be misled, we must understand that the path toward awakening should be considered as a path of initiation. Since the West forms the centre of our pre-occupations, we will now consider more closely the Western spiritual path.

'I am the Way, the Truth and the Life', Jesus said, linking the three aspects of a single Reality. The first Christians spoke of their faith as a 'way' or a 'path'.

The sage Lao Tzu united the precepts of Chinese wisdom into the 'Tao', which signifies the 'Way'. The Kato Indians called the first man 'Nagaico', the great traveller, mediator between the diurnal path of the sun and the nocturnal path of the moon.

We are travellers on earth, and our movement is horizontal. However, in the course of our evolution, our aspirations rise vertically. The image of a cross symbolizes the horizontal and vertical paths of the traveller and evokes the idea of a migratory soul rising above existence, suggesting thereby the idea of reincarnation. On a more mundane level, our horizontal movement is linked to the attraction we feel for vast open space which invites us to travel out of sheer love of movement.

Therefore, since time immemorial we have explored our universe, and today we probe space and land on the moon.

A great number of youngsters set out with their knapsacks on their backs to seek truth afar, not realizing that it can be found deep within themselves.

In the Middle Ages, whoever wanted to learn a trade had first to be accepted by a master in apprenticeship, and finally had to travel several years as a journeyman.

Through the links established among these journey-men, trades developed and the travelling craftsmen con-stituted an evolutionary element on many levels.

The French Revolution destroyed this established order and wanderers replaced the journeymen. Wander-ing is not harmful in itself, but it lacks the support of tradition as an aid in finding one's way.

When we examine the path of the West, we are con-fronted by the mystery of how, where and when it was chosen by Western travellers. Let us enter the path at the moment where it reaches a peak.

There, we find the master of Samos radiant in his authority. In his inner courtyard, the Esoteria, Pythagoras teaches that Evolution is the Law of Life, that Number is the Law of the Universe and that Unity is the Law of God. Let us meet Apollo, the solar god, symbol of beauty, master of rhythm, and master of the seventh portal guarding the secrets of the universe and its rhythm. When we speak of rhythm, we evoke frequency, and when we evoke frequency, we hint at numbers.

We may recall that the world owes its harmony to the vibration of the seven-stringed lyre of the solar god, and we may remember that he has a brother Dionysus, whose importance equals his own.

The mysteries of Eleusis were consecrated to Dionysus, the cosmic spirit of nature and the guide of souls seeking the divine Light, as well as to Demeter, the 'da-mater' or mother earth, meaning its goddess.

It was Orpheus who created the mysteries of Eleusis. The Great Orphic Tradition sought to reveal a path of wisdom allowing those initiated into its mysteries to discover cosmic harmony so that they might work in full awareness of the plan of evolution, free from all illusion, helping everything progress towards perfection.

Let us realize that today the past, like the serpent of fire symbolized by the torchbearers in the great Eleusinian night, reaches us in concentric spirals to remind us that everything existing is rooted in what has been and is the foundation for what is yet to come.

Let us admire Pericles, builder of the Acropolis, and the tragedies of Aeschylus, hero of the battles of Marathon and Salamis, where a small nation overcame a great empire.

Let us revere Sophocles and his tragedies and the perfection of Zeno's logic. Let us listen to Socrates who taught his students how to engage in dialogue, and let us admire him when he states to his judges: 'I do not defend myself for my own sake, as one might believe, but for love of you, fearing that you would offend God in condemning me.'

Socrates was followed by Plato and Aristotle. Let us not forget in this brief overview Melissos, Empedocles, Anaxagoras and Democritus, the first atomist, as well as a host of other philosophers whose thoughts remain alive.

The Greek miracle prepared the way for the Christian revelation. Jesus announced that although men were of divine origin, they neglected the kingdom of God by failing to love one another.

He paid for his audacity on the cross, but Christianity perpetuated his message.

Centuries passed; the Church decreed what should be believed, and Christians persecuted other Christians. However, Christian charity spread and the sense of justice penetrated human institutions.

Science triumphed and, forgetting that science was of our own making, we attributed to it possibilities which exceeded its competence. Consequently, we began to fear it.

At certain turning points in history, we must claim our

legacy, if only to give expression to what is inherent in the existing order.

In full awareness of its past, the West should make use of its attitude, its influence and its determination to fulfil its vocation. It should defend eternal values so that they may form the foundation for authentic progress.

There is no need to predict an imminent cataclysm. The West's technological and scientific methods and its wealth are quite sufficient to accomplish its mission. Clearly, the notion of profit for profit's sake must be abolished and replaced by notions which enhance well-Being. We must also accept the fact that the desire to work less, to consume more, to claim more rights and to close our eyes to the obvious, hoping that a horn of plenty will pour its riches on to the world, is not an attitude worthy of a thinking human being.

Only a lucid perception of the links making the world a coherent and interdependent whole will bring forth the necessary solutions, which then must be applied in accordance with local traditions and regional conditions. Otherwise, human advancement may be jeopardized.

National sensitivities, ethnic strife, racial conflicts and greed on all sides constitute serious obstacles. It is not always easy to convince others, and it is also risky to impose appropriate solutions by force, even provisionally.

Risk must sometimes be accepted in order to achieve a just distribution of the world's wealth instead of the exploitation practised by an array of profiteers, petty kings or 'democratically' chosen dictators who have usurped the positions left behind by former colonists.

Every equitable distribution is based upon a sense of shared responsibility, which must serve as a criterion for the way in which wealth is distributed. Each remuneration will then be proportional to the responsibilities assumed at a particular level of the hierarchy. Needless to say, the equitable remuneration should not be imposed by law but freely accepted as being fair. It is important to recognize this, since it makes freedom of choice possible and underlines the importance of freely accepted responsibility.

We may also state that in the proper meaning of the term, order is never linked to any kind of power. Order is the law which indicates the path to follow. The means used to create favourable conditions for the development of the population will form the foundation for a civilization which invites the awakened human being to think and act correctly in order to assume his human vocation in full dignity.

CHAPTER 21

Intellectual Ideologists

Evolution implies a creative dynamism, a universal energy which seems to obey a guiding impulse. The interactions of all phenomena manifesting themselves in the universe at a particular moment determine and bear within them the seed of the future.

The cosmic order reflects an Intelligence-Consciousness which leads to progress made possible by experience on all levels of manifestation. Forms disappear, giving birth to new forms better adapted to the requirements of the movement of Life, thereby establishing the thread linking the ephemeral to the eternal.

Everything evolves, either by an extremely slow transformation or by a sometimes abrupt mutation when surrounding conditions vary suddenly so that a critical point is reached.

Evolution is a fact accepted by modern science. However, its mechanism is not well understood.

Evolution makes it possible to perceive the dynamism which pulsates in all things. To understand its law is to submit to it.

In the new age the awakened human being who has become aware of the mission of the West – based upon a tradition indicating a path of action illuminated by

Intelligence-Consciousness – should reach another level of comprehension. In the midst of the convulsions of a world on the edge of an abyss, we must discover a path of salvation which we can follow.

If humanity is deprived of a path of action, on all levels we may become lost amidst arbitrary notions based upon vague observations. These notions may serve the needs of the moment, but if they are perpetuated, they become obstacles to a progression which requires the constant expansion of Cognizance.

Expansion is the result of an understanding facilitated by symbols, which transmit universal messages in their secret language.

Jupiter and his thunderbolt symbolize omnipotent Energy. The caduceus carried by Hermes evokes the Tree of Life around which are entwined two serpents representing the two opposing energies, the active and passive, illustrating the two poles of manifestation which, while in apparent opposition, are in fact complementary.

These are only two random examples. Man, representing the summit of evolution on earth, has developed civilizations which throughout the ages have served as a foundation for his existence. Therefore, today he must pay attention to the foundation he will leave to his children, whose requirements will correspond to those of the age of Aquarius.

The civilization of the new age requires a different approach to human problems, as well as solutions which are more appropriate to humanity's spiritual, scientific or physical needs.

The West is seeking its path unable to discern the ways and means leading to a new vision of a fraternal civilization.

Ideas conflict with one another, clashing periodically

with each other in familiar patterns which produce the same results as in the past. It is time to abandon them in order to discover our destiny and the reason for our evolution.

Because it lacks a notion of Being, which in fact is difficult to define, the West has chosen a false realism, an arbitrary elaboration of theories and systems.

Idealism, pragmatism, positivism and materialism are only a minor part of these elaborations, which crystallize opinions and subject individuals to the despotism of ideas.

Mental associations of ideas have given birth to worship of the intellect which has as its 'god' efficiency based upon ideology.

Perhaps it would be more appropriate to speak of the 'efficient action' of ideology in military, social, political, technical, religious or other spheres, where it galvanizes crowds.

The god placed on a pedestal by intellectual ideologists is responsible for the chain reactions of history. Everyone is asked to accept ideologies so that these reactions may continue to the benefit of those who established them. George Bernard Shaw once commented that 'the reasonable individual adapts himself to circumstances, whereas the unreasonable one wants to adapt circumstances to his own requirements.' We are unreasonable!

Such folly is contagious, and the mental errors of even well-intentioned persons can be attributed to these circumstances, since many consider it legitimate to restrict individual liberties in order to force others into the mould of ideologies which serve the interests of a particular social class.

Forgetful that liberty is the essence of spirit, and therefore of all civilization, these individuals undermine humanism as an expression of great originality which might develop to the point of genius and which can only be conceived in full liberty.

This Primordial Liberty is ridiculed because it threatens class structure, needed to justify class struggles. Conflict spreads and war looms on the horizon. Such reactions lead to fanaticism and to dogmatism, bringing about confusion in the world. It is because of our mental confusion that we consider thought to be sufficient unto itself, although we fail to understand what thought is.

Psychological dualism, based upon the notion that the thinker is separate from his thought, has greatly contributed to the individual's submission to theories, dogmas and systems.

The thinker, considering thought to be the panacea of all ills, and eager to make use of it for his own practical needs, confers upon ideas a tyrannical power which influences the human environment. Despite the failures illustrated by contemporary history, doctrines continue to survive and individuals accept the edicts of ideology out of habit, lack of initiative or inertia.

Within the limits of their assumptions, they strengthen intellectualism and lend credence to the concept of historical materialism, which produces a society of human beings unaware of their true possibilities.

A human being who is unaware of his true nature does not count for much in the world dominated by abstractions – that is, by ideas detached from the thinkers who engendered them. We are asked to cherish these abstractions rather than to develop our individuality. Logic, conceived in this way, implies the willingness to submit to a rigorous discipline imposed by such abstraction.

If we are to avoid creating a society of human beings unaware of their potential, if we are to help the world move towards a better understanding of humanity and its evolution, if we are to find solutions to human problems, then we must affirm that man exists and thinks as a 'Being'.

Therefore, we should revise the famous Cartesian statement: 'I think; therefore I am', so that it is more appropriate for the new age: '*I think: therefore I exist. But beyond the thought produced by my brain, which is subject to a variety of physical, psychological and spiritual impressions, I am.*'

If we accept this statement, we will become aware that we are prisoners of a host of existential, emotional, illusory or materialist reactions, and therefore victims of a loss of freedom resulting from a lack of confidence in the Self.

By establishing a harmoniously balanced relationship between existential requirements and the aspirations of our authentic Being, between the constraints of daily existence and the dreams of our innermost Self, we will understand that Truth and Life guide our evolution, which is meant to unfold for our well-Being while maintaining in proper balance our physical, psychological and spiritual universes.

Since they are unaware that well-Being is not synonymous with 'existing well,' nations pursue incoherent policies and adopt political, economic and social systems which are out of harmony with the decisions which Intelligence-Consciousness would make if it were allowed to become the leading factor of existence.

Today, theories, systems and dogmas no longer correspond to the aspirations of a generation in search of something quite different, even if the seekers do not understand what that implies.

Many forms of government seem anachronistic and are only maintained by improvisations or by force. They are no longer adapted to the contemporary world, in which scholars and researchers discover the unity of the universe through their different scientific, intellectual or spiritual investigations.

Sooner or later, these scholars and researchers will become convinced that Primordial Liberty is the leaven in a world of which man is an integral conscious part, responsible for his choice. Only man and the mystery he carries within him can provide the key to his reality, which requires an appropriate social, political and religious expression not imposed by ideology, but corresponding to what he essentially is.

Therefore, we may conclude this study of the foundations of a civilization based upon well-Being by investigating the mystery of man, his purpose and his evolution.

Since civilization is impossible if human beings do not know themselves well, self-knowledge must become an accepted factor in everyday life. The key to the problem is to be found at this level.

As long as the individual, either alone or as part of a group and its ideology, deludes himself in order to justify his thoughts, actions or reactions, or those of his group, conflict in all its forms will prevail.

CHAPTER 22

Know Thyself

If we are to create a civilization which fosters our evolution, and therefore competence, a collaboration of the different branches of activity – professional, scientific or artistic – is required so that human genius may develop at all levels.

A harmonious environment is required for human qualities to be awakened, and only human qualities should serve as the foundation for a viable society.

Moreover, it is by practising a trade, pursuing a profession, developing an inventive spirit, and refining our capacity for initiative and our sense of solidarity that we can progress.

From the knowledge we have of ourselves, we develop a discipline which fosters our self-realization and our integration into society. We can then inspire others without imposing ourselves on them, unless we have the ability to become a leader.

Group collaboration for the accomplishment of a task relies upon a hierarchy of values, manifested by each individual. An example of such a collaboration and of such a hierarchy is provided by a theatrical production.

The playwright represents the pinnacle of the hierarchy. On the next level, the director respects the spirit of the work without, however, neglecting his own genius, which enables him to develop an interpretation faithful to the author's intentions.

He chooses actors receptive to his vision of the work and he conceives the most appropriate stage sets, which designers, machinists and electricians will then create under his guidance.

The entire team, from the costume designer to the make-up artist, understand the meaning of the work and collaborate to make it perfect. They will share as a group in the success.

If we transpose this example into daily life, the task of teachers, professors, parents and leaders in any educational field – sociological, scientific, economic or political – should be to render perceptible the impressive work accomplished by individuals aware of their role and their abilities.

In order for a common endeavour to be creative, all the collaborators must feel involved, and the effort of each one should be respected. The team spirit must not be limited to the professional domain, but should expand further to make possible the birth of masterpieces created for the glory of civilization.

This is merely a vision of how the world might be, but in these turbulent times tyrannized by ideology, we must endeavour to make it a reality. Human beings must become aware of the idea of collaboration, which can create conditions permitting the expression of liberty and happiness on earth.

Is this an original idea? Can we say that there is nothing new under the sun, when the massive and accelerating movement of evolution and the urgency of world problems cause confusion and arouse fear? In a world full of conflict and anxiety, in a world where anguished man upsets the social order, where the upset order disturbs the nation and the disturbed nation intensifies the conflict, can we aspire to a fundamental change if we claim that similar efforts have already been made in vain?

We must abandon the vicious circle and cease referring to the failures of the past, which have no relevance to the present!

Rules, laws, customs and behaviour depend upon human values. Human values must be allowed to emerge as we abandon false notions reinforced by emotionality, education, propaganda, impulsive reactions or the influence of the environment – in brief, by the conditioning which is accepted in the place of freedom.

All conditioning is an obstacle to the manifestation of Intelligence which must be unencumbered if we are to penetrate behind facts and events in order to sift out the essential, without allowing any mental projection to interfere.

Unfortunately, even when extended by ultra-sophisticated instruments, our senses can only perceive a limited universe, in the macrocosm as well as in the microcosm. Human psychological structures are not suited for penetrating the essence of things, unless they are receptive to the most subtle impulses which can only be perceived in the calmness of a mind at rest.

But the mind is confused, since imagination has great power and multiplies the endless difficulties of existence, producing a feeling of dissatisfaction and frustration.

In our daily activities we maintain such feelings of insecurity and dissatisfaction, which lead to frustration. Therefore, we feel the need to escape and to seek satisfaction, imagining that by attaining it we will be able to discover certainties which can deliver us from all fear.

Seeking satisfaction, we also hope to enjoy the pleasures of existence. This encourages us to escape headlong into reassuring illusions.

Thus we imagine a heaven inhabited by a father so great that he knows everything, sees everything and is capable of doing anything. Obviously, we try to be in his good graces, persuading ourselves that the mere outward appearance of virtuous behaviour will satisfy him.

Poor limited human beings that we are, unaware that our belief in him might, by reaction, lead to disbelief or, worse yet, to worship of the devil, his opposite!

Caught in a dilemma, we can resolve it by making the wise decision to become conscious of a reality accessible to those who have transcended their conceptual limits.

Then wisdom is revealed and love can be expressed. Wisdom commands us, as already stated, to know ourselves without judgement, without justification and without condemnation. Such is the sole path to discernment. Then Intelligence, stripped of the veils of intellectual, political, social or ideological conditioning, can replace confusion, especially confusion of thought. Confused thought attempts to find satisfaction and reassurance, which are nothing more than mental projections.

We may claim to be united with everything, failing to realize that this claim is an existential embroidery of a confused mind, nothing more than a subterfuge. We are playing with Maya, an element of deception. We act 'as if', and abandon ourselves to illusion.

Sitting cross-legged at the foot of Mont Blanc, we would be mistaken if we imagined that our good intentions can cause Maya, the great illusion, to carry us to the summit so that we might experience the satisfaction of having attained it without the necessary effort.

Great indeed would be the satisfaction of being able to boast about something which we have undeservedly achieved. We might even claim to have received a just reward which was our due.

Following the path of authentic self-realization, we

must abandon ambitious dreams which arouse widely accepted illusions carefully maintained because of the satisfaction they provide.

No, nothing is new under the sun, even if the problems change in dimension. However, we may also state that the experiences of the past, as well as the failures and sufferings which accompany them, contain the seed of change.

To understand this enables us to cross the threshold guarded by the Sphinx, a symbol of the great mystery of Life.

Let us not be afraid to face the problems which must be solved!

CHAPTER 23

The Choice

We must have the vision of the Eternal in order to see things as they are in their essence. We lack the vision of the Eternal because, imprisoned in a structured psychological universe, we are only interested in whatever happens within the framework of our limits.

We only conceive of things in proportion to these limits, and we claim to organize our individual, physical and intellectual lives according to concepts which are shaped to suit our prison.

Nevertheless, we pretend that the type of organization we have established reflects the cosmic harmony, without realizing that we have created an element of opposition out of the contradictions inherent in our pretensions.

Although we long to transcend whatever constrains us, we refuse to free ourselves. We might say with Maeterlinck that our dream is to be a passer-by who would not pass by.

But the passer-by who does not want to pass by suffers from a permanent inner contradiction. His suffering is the cause of his urgent need for certainty in all domains of thought; he therefore creates for himself an artificial certainty which he uses to destroy contradiction. Passionately he defends this artificial certainty and passionately he represses the contradiction by attacking the contradictor, whom he will not hesitate to destroy in order to reinforce his certainty.

Despite cleverly presented justifications, this behaviour is more akin to barbarism than to civilization.

Confronted with the spectacle of carnage, murder, torture, rape and orgies perpetrated by those who call themselves civilized, we might be tempted to say that civilization is as close to barbarism as polished iron is to rust: a drop of water is sufficient to make it appear.

Civilization, addressing the individual of the new age, might plead: 'Care for me well: I am your safeguard! Barbarism is a state to which I easily revert when you stop offering me your attentions and your care, which can make me a living reality. Heed my words and do not forget what I am going to tell you. It is the respect you give to Intelligence-Consciousness and to the Love which it generates that allows my gifts to flourish. Gather today the roses of destiny, whose subtle perfumes grace the paths leading to revelation. Your happiness depends on it.'

Constant upheavals cause us to abandon the belief that one day we might attain happiness. However, the mission of the West is to transform such universal anguish into hope. This conclusion indicates the choice which has to be made. Decline or renewal.

Let us summarize the reasons justifying this hope.

Conclusion

We are living in a century which gives us access to energies surrounding us, penetrating us, informing us.

These omnipresent energies pervade space and remind us of the interdependence of humanity in all parts of the world.

However, an anachronism persists: our thinking and reasoning rely upon outdated concepts and on antiquated notions which define our problems in terms of egocentric preoccupations.

We believe in rigid systems and we think that everything can be described by 'yes' or 'no', by 'good' or 'bad'.

Our habits of thought make us follow customary patterns leading to conclusions we hope to make logical, despite the fact that the assumptions upon which they are based have not been verified.

In our electronic world of waves and vibrations, the ever-shifting relationship of the individual to the ambient world should expand his horizons, bringing him closer to his neighbour in a common understanding, encouraging him to transcend his own intellectual limits.

In fact, today more than ever, our opinions divide us, our dogmas are in conflict and our theories pit believers against non-believers in outdated political, social or demagogic strife.

We seek rational knowledge, specialization and possessions, when today more than ever we need to understand and to expand our comprehension.

The new dimension called 'time' has upset our formerly static world. Our psychological development necessarily rejects a standardized technological society and its automation, which makes us slaves of the bureaucratic organization hemming in our existence.

Only someone who uses all his faculties in his work as well as in his leisure is able to stop running away from himself and to stop distracting himself in order to kill time.

Only by discovering outlets for our creative forces appropriate to our abilities, and only by developing our psychological faculties so as to fulfil our evolution, can we follow the one path which will lead us out of the labyrinth of confusion which threatens to destroy us.

If we fail to recognize that such an evolution is essential, that it requires an authentic humanism, and that it is rooted in the deepest part of ourselves, we misunderstand our destiny and we betray it.

On this level, we are all more or less accomplices!

When we betray our destiny and therefore our mission, we are riding the tragic toboggan down the slope made ever more slippery by our ignorance.

It is difficult for us to remain true to our destiny, since in order to do so we must be available, which means free: free from all pre-established concepts, free from all preconceived opinions, free ultimately from all psychological conditioning.

Human beings are caught in the turmoil of existence and, amidst its turbulence, they find themselves trapped by events for which they incorrectly believe they are not responsible. Consequently, they blame chance, bad luck, misfortune.

Chance is a convenient word. According to circumstances, it can be unfortunate or providential. It can be feared or cajoled; but is this not a useless effort? Does this treacherous or providential chance really exist?

In the early period of its use, the word 'chance' was linked to the word 'game'. But nowadays we prefer to give it a different interpretation.

If a snag develops between apparent causes and anticipated effects, we attribute it to chance.

This is a lazy attitude, since it encourages us to persevere in our ignorance of the true causes which have produced an unexpected effect.

The occurrence of unforeseen effects does not imply that indeterminism exists or that capriciousness plays a role in the order of things.

An effect quite simply results from an interference of multiple forces, certain of which escape our observation. Many threads are needed to weave a cloth. It is the same with the web which determines the events affecting us.

In our attempt to discover the threads, we must not cut the Gordian knots tied by our unconscious, which reflect what has been suppressed. Instead, we should recognize and thereby dissolve them.

The free human being can and must choose his path. This choice must be an intelligent one. 'Intellegere' means to understand, and to understand means to discover a truth which remains perfectly accessible at all levels of consciousness, provided that this truth is approached with a calm mind and an open spirit.

Then good and evil are merely part of an existential development which the awakened, free individual embraces without preconceptions, without mental projections and without concern for apparent pheno-mena which falsify his judgement.

He is aware that he is acting in accordance with a vocation which it is his destiny to accomplish.

The psychologically free individual is not attached to his assumptions, even if they are momentarily valid. He accepts the fact that he must die each moment to his habits. He enlarges his sphere of understanding, realiz-ing that human nature finds its fundamental essence when it is free from egotism and from the ignorance which debases it.

Without fear and without blame, he learns to confront the obscure forces which limit him. He becomes a con-scious actor on the stage of the world. He intervenes in the show, but does not allow himself to be caught in it.

Amidst the feverish turmoil of the world, he knows the rules of the existential game. They require him to give equal consideration to pleasure and pain, to gain and loss, to victory and defeat. When he understands these rules, he accepts the existential duality manifested in all things, but he accepts it only at the level of a game.

The conscious human being is free to withdraw from the green baize table around which the game of existence is played, and to remain aloof from the fray. However, he can also choose to consider it as a field of experience which fosters his evolution.

An anchorite can find the path of truth in an isolated cave. In the activity of the world, the discovery of our path is certainly much more difficult, but our personal experience illustrates the profound longing of our Being to manifest itself and to create in daily life the harmony so difficult to achieve amidst the struggles of humanity.

The Law which governs human beings impels them toward such harmony, which unites opposites by trans-cending them. To violate this harmony is to betray our vocation, and this fundamental betrayal is not pardonable. We are inevitably its victims. It is useless to blame chance or a mysterious force which pursues us; the apparent injustice is only an illusion. We are ignoring the process which unravels the tangled web of links, which may, if such an eventuality is taken into account, have been woven in successive existences. All evil comes from our ignorance, which cannot be dissipated by mere knowledge.

A great master of the Himalayas once wrote to one of his disciples that evil in itself does not exist. He added: 'All evil, great or small, is in human action, in man who is, because of his intelligence, the sole free agent in nature.'

It is man who invented false gods to justify all his subterfuges and to allow him to commit all sorts of crimes on the pretext that such is the will of the gods.

Nature is neither good nor evil. It simply follows immutable laws, either providing life and joy or sending suffering and death and destroying her creations. We must not blame nature nor an imaginary divinity, but rather human nature degraded by egotism.

Behind an opaque veil, egotism hides from us the Beautiful, the True and the Good. Our quest for power leads us astray. Only suffering calls us back to order.

Although we are filled with good intentions, we attach great value to our desires, our possessions, our beliefs. We prefer not to understand. We accuse fate. We deplore our bad luck. We blame those who fail to understand us. We wage war against our fellow human beings in order to justify the unjustifiable.

The mission of the West, if it is to have a meaning, should be to promote the understanding that all individuals from every nation on earth belong to the human family.

This is not merely a statement. It is also a definition emphasizing the importance of fraternal understanding in creating respect for the particular character of each individual.

Respect invites us to defend any individual or group of individuals oppressed in the name of any ideology or régime. Respect for the individual must prevail, and prejudice must not be allowed to establish differences which might be beneficial or harmful to one group or another.

In this way a supremely human tradition will be created for the benefit of all, giving priority to human values and respecting individual rights and liberties in the name of these values.

The vast range of experience offered by the world is available to us, provided we accept it. Day after day we must seek the Philosopher's Stone, and the Tao reminds us that our body serves as a cup in which to distil, drop by drop, our own immortality.

If we neglect the Great Work, if we allow ourselves to be led astray by sensual pleasures, then these pleasures will devour us.

When their attractions have paled, we will look into a mirror, and the despair of our wasted existence will be the companion of our disillusion. In vain we will seek support from others.

The hostile world, as selfish as we have been, will ignore us.

In our bitterness, we will prostrate ourselves, exclaiming, 'Did I deserve this?' And no answer will come from the silent gods.

Is it not wiser to embark upon the great adventure, admitting that the 'Lord of Heaven can express himself through man on earth', as Saint Paul has said? We can become the channels of this expression and thereby experience the ineffable joy of fulfilling our destiny, conscious of our stature and of our mission, conscious also that true understanding promotes Love, which resolves all conflicts.

May a new Renaissance prove that those prophets who take pleasure in predicting imminent disasters are mistaken.

If these must occur, let us contemplate them calmly. That is the best way to avoid them!